Finite Perfection

Finite Perfection

Reflections on Virtue

Michael A. Weinstein

The University of Massachusetts Press   Amherst, 1985

Library of Congress Cataloging in Publication Data
Weinstein, Michael A.
Finite perfection.
Includes index.
1. Ethics.   2. Virtues.   I. Title.
BJ1012.W38   1985   179'.9   84–16215
ISBN 0–87023–474–9
ISBN 0–87023–475–7 (pbk.)

To Deena, in freedom

Contents

Introduction   1

1 A Context for the Virtues   9

2 Self-Control   47

3 Artistry   87

4 Love   125

Envoi   161

Name Index   165

Subject Index   167

Introduction

Does the work to follow need an explanation, an introduction?
It is a philosophical essay, perhaps a meditation, written in a
free style, drawing upon an experience of several years of trying to come to terms with what emerged within myself and
what I then began to push to extremities to overcome—that is,
evil and joy, evil with joy, in all their phases. The essay should
speak for itself. Introductions only make things simpler, providing readers and especially reviewers with "finger posts," as
Samuel Alexander called them. But let me plant some, nonetheless, so that you might find your way more easily to where I
would lead you with a suspect hand. Although you will not need
them, they might prove useful to me, inasmuch as even a crafted
text is a wilderness.

Evil—which is always present in a personal existent, an individuated human being, because we suffer so many adversities
so deeply and delight so extravagantly (the latter if we can succeed in letting ourselves)—first obtruded into my awareness
more than a decade ago when one day I heard the voice of a
beast in me, a savage who did not want to die, to get sick, to
grow old, and who did not want to miss out on ecstasy. Disturb-

ing panic and high desire, these two ripped apart the com-
promises I had prepared so carefully and calculatedly to secure
me as a social being in an organizational society. The beast was
loose, and then came the project of taming it, still incomplete,
but sufficiently advanced to indicate where it would have to
conclude if it could ever be successful (and it cannot be—there
is no cure for adversity, and I choose not to renounce at least
some excess). The struggle to tame the beast ends, for me, with
virtue, strictly individualized virtue that organizes artistry and
love around self-control.

But I should dwell on evil a bit in this introduction, because
that is where the trouble began. There will be enough later on
overcoming—if, indeed, there can be such a thing. Evil, as I have
felt it, takes two forms. The first, let us call it the greater evil
of the Manichaean sort, springs from our response to adversity,
which is always on a declivity toward hatred for existence, which
issues in the kind of rebellion associated with Ivan Karamazov
and the Underground Man. The hatred for existence is destructive and nihilistic, hearkening back to Sigmund Freud's Thanatos
and Friedrich Nietzsche's "denial of life." That one wants so
much to live and be happy (what is there to be ashamed of?),
both of which are not possible, the latter, at least, on the whole,
breeds the will to annihilate the broken totality drenched in
frustration. The essay to follow takes for granted that the hatred
for existence has been brought under some control (a very
large assumption), because only in light of a joy in finite perfections, in limited delights, can one speak of a virtuous life.
Virtue conquers, at least for some moments, the hatred for
existence, but it can only do so when that hatred is a bit on the
wane; a fruitful paradox. All virtue depends on an affirmation
of finite and flawed life. Any attempt to make it depend on
anything else secretes evil, usually in the form of Nietzsche's
ressentiment, the symptom of repression. Greater evil is abated
without repression by what William James called "inward

tolerance," that is, by allowing hatred to be imaginatively represented with all of its emotional power. It is further abated by applying Irving Babbitt's "inner check" to forestall its overt release. In time self-control is strengthened sufficiently to make the inner check nearly a habit—perhaps through such disciplines as psychoanalysis (interpreted simply as free association on the material of imagination) and the Eastern art of sitting.

Even if one has achieved some success in containing the hatred of existence and its overt manifestations, evil still has a foothold. We are not merely hopelessly frustrated by adversity, but we also have life-affirming desires that run to excess and can easily ruin us. Undisciplined appetites are at the core of the lesser evil of the Augustinian sort. So close are they to the affirmation of life that it is not even clear that they should be overcome, as I believe that greater evil should be strenuously fought. There is always the question, for those who attempt to act out of themselves, of whether or not to satisfy a claimant desire that has spread over life its pathetic fallacy of bliss—a fallacy, indeed, but one that results in real, though severely restricted, satisfactions. What to do about pleasure—which disturbs the good order of the fictions and functions we call social life—is the unresolved question of the following essay. And pleasure disturbs not only social designs (that is serious enough), but also that network of personal loyalties and allegiances necessary to exercising the virtues of artistry and love. So, I come down on the side of self-control, both for its own sake as a liberation of the self and for the sake of mastery over things and free service to other selves. Self-control, artistry, and love all bind time and alleviate the lesser evil, the torment of strife among limited goods, the brutality of excess. But I am not so sure of myself. I cling to a Dionysian counterpoint to an Apollonian theme. The moment of abandon, the upsurge of the delighted beast, a solipsist seeking union, is something I choose not to efface. Does that shatter virtue?

As I understand it, virtue is thoroughly individual. One first brings oneself under control by acknowledging the full array of one's desires and fears, inhibiting the release of those rooted in hatred, and accepting one's own transgressions; and then one moves on to self-conscious mastery of the arts of living well and to devoting oneself to serving particular other persons in a spirit of free commitment. Here my discussion sets up an alternative to another recent reflection, that of Alasdair MacIntyre in *After Virtue: A Study in Moral Theory* (Notre Dame: University of Notre Dame Press, 1982). MacIntyre poses the choice: Nietzsche or Aristotle. He opts for the latter and works out a moral theory based on virtue-in-community. This is the nub of his thesis: "For if the conception of a good has to be expounded in terms of such actions as those of a practice, of the narrative unity of a human life and of a moral tradition, then goods, and with them the only grounds for the authority of laws and virtues, can only be discovered by entering into those relationships which constitute communities whose central bond is a shared vision of an understanding of goods" (p. 240). MacIntyre finds monstrous the possibility of the Nietzschian man who "has a solitude within him that is inaccessible to praise or blame, his own justice that is beyond appeal." I simply do not find it monstrous; rather, it is such solitude, I call it "radical separation," that grounds the possibility of affirming finite life. How can I dispute MacIntyre? I do not deny such classical virtues as temperance, courage, and justice. I just find the beast within me and I seek to tame it and to release it. That demands a personal discipline; anything else might come later. But one might also wonder whether self-control might be a liver option, in William James's sense, than tradition in the Weberian world that both MacIntyre and I believe we inhabit. For one who suffers from hatred and excess, the call to moderation rings very hollow; that to community barely sounds at all.

I choose Nietzsche over Aristotle, but not MacIntyre's Nietzsche, who holds that values and morals are a function of subjective will. I do not believe, as MacIntyre argues, that the Aristotelian tradition fell victim to modernity; rather, it was challenged decisively by Augustine and before him by Paul of Tarsus. Thus, Nietzsche is not, for me, MacIntyre's standard textbook case, who ushers in a relativism based on will, the last modern enmeshed in the modern; he is the contemporary Augustine strained through Machiavelli and Rousseau, the exponent of a *virtù* that is deeply in touch with the sense of molten life. My Nietzsche is the one who set himself the task of overcoming *ressentiment,* of affirming finite and finally isolated and individuated life, personal existence. That Nietzsche is not a partisan of liberalism *in extremis,* but of self-control in the service of joy. Post-Augustinian man is one who has taken himself to heart and is, therefore, dangerous to community. His selfishness is overwhelming and often leads to self-destruction, the antidote to frustration. I take Max Weber seriously when he says that the great problem of modern life is to learn how to tolerate routine with good grace. That is a prior problem, for me, to the traditional ones on which MacIntyre subsists. Need the selfish one be dangerous to the other selves within his ken? Augustine thought he would have to be malign, and so he took the desperate expedient of deliverance, of faith, which meant repression. It is faith that has been eroded in our world, not tradition; it is far too easy to say tradition. We now live with the return of what Augustine repressed, of the fleshly, passionate, self-loving and self-centered, frustrated beast, the animal as we know it from within, not the "political animal" known to the moral "theorist." At least I live with the beast and, to follow the good physician of Nietzsche's *Daybreak,* one who has heard the beast's call might well read the following essay as a prolegomenon to MacIntyre's reflections. Thought has something in it of medicine and there are no panaceas. What I offer here is the possibility that in the absence of tradition, virtue may take the place of faith, at least for some people; we might become less dangerous to one another and, so much to claim, enjoy each other's company more.

My defense of personal virtue appears in the face of a society that is rapidly becoming altogether impersonal. The most significant social process operating today in American society, and probably in all Western societies, is what I call the "externalization of the mind." In a society made up primarily of complex organizations guided, officially, by technical rationality and subservient to the aims of profit and power, all human activities tend to become functions—that is, chains of overt occurrences that can be described precisely and that eventuate, under specific conditions, in determinate and predictable results. Technical rationality rose to predominance as a form of social intelligence in the machine age, and now we are witnessing the mechanization of the mind, the invasion of the machine not only into calculative thought but into the formation of the sensibility through such media as television and psychotropic drugs. The grand public problem of modernity—how to unify a diversity of individuals engaging in far-flung relations that prohibit their direct acquaintance with one another—is being approached through the strategy of substituting technical constraint for voluntary solidarity. If we can engineer social spaces such that everyone is secure in performing their functions, we will have attained a world in which personal virtue is superfluous, if not subversive. But mechanization seems to have its limits: as the technical order becomes more rationalized, the beast is pushed further out into the open, demanding vengeance and pleasure. And then personal virtue is at a premium: it becomes not only the sole defense against enslavement to organizational designs (and for many it may be a curse to have such a defense), but also the very foundation of personality. But should personality—the disciplined expression of a unique center of living imagination— be desired? In the organizational society it is to be replaced by licensed competence and programmed pleasure. And that is another choice, one already made for most people.

The vision of a society exhausted by fictions and functions is the bad dream lurking at the borders of American classical philosophy. The following essay was preceded by two books, *The Wilderness and the City,* in which I investigated the life-philosophies of Josiah Royce, Charles Sanders Peirce, William James, John Dewey, and George Santayana; and *Unity and Variety in the Philosophy of Samuel Alexander.* It was in my examination of the American classical thinkers that I found the basis for the individualism that marks my freer reflections here. Confronted by the hatred of existence, which took for them the dual form of the "war spirit" seeking to impose impossible demands on the world, and *acedia,* the despairing slackness of will, the American thinkers counseled both deliverance to an ideal community and an inward tolerance of life. Through the first they hoped to set up an alternative to what Irving Babbitt called the "efficient megalomania" of modern industrialism, whereas the second provided an internal check on it. I believe it is too late in the process of the externalization of the mind to take the social prescription seriously; even if it were not too late, the appeal to community is only compelling if individuals are virtuous. Otherwise bureaucracy might provide a better context for the affirmation of life, if only because it contrasts so sharply with it. The prescription for the individual, inward tolerance, however, is the core of the founding virtue of self-control, which makes the present work part of an American discourse. The appeal to personal virtue is the homegrown antidote to American technicism.

My work on the twentieth-century British philosopher Samuel Alexander supplied the basis for the virtue of artistry, which builds upon self-control to extend the affirmation of life into the transformation of circumstances into goods. In Alexander's later work on the philosophy of art I found implicit the vision of

an Apollonian civilization in which constructive activity would
be interpreted through the finite perfections it created. For
Alexander each art is a mixture of mind and material, an in-
formed content that has a particular criterion of achievement,
even if, as in the case of the fine arts, that criterion is specific to
a unique work. The idea of a civilization that self-consciously
acknowledges finitude and yet seeks perfection within its bounds
would be the public fruition of personal virtue. But even that
would not be enough, because artistry is ruthless and ignores
the individual selves for whom it is undertaken. It is love that
crowns the personal virtues, a paradoxical love that acknowledges "the otherness of the other," the radical separation of each
one, and still serves so that the other can be free. A stern and
yet joyful love that ever fails but persistently returns is the
unique contribution of this work, if it be thought a contribution
at all in a world in which we would be pleased so much to have
the luxury of being Thomas Paine's "summer soldiers and sun-
shine patriots" for each other and to leave winter and darkness
to the machines.

1   A Context for the Virtues

Philosophy reposes on a base of what has generally been regarded as religious experience, though it would be more appropriate here to call it (after Henri Bergson) synoptic vision. In turn, the context of vision or the overall sense of life is psychology, understood as the project of describing precisely the structure of experience as it is known to the inward gaze of an individual human self, or, to put it more abstractly, of an individuated life. If it is vision that provides the experience on which philosophy works, and psychology that discovers the structure of experience by analyzing it into its primary components—that is, apparently irreducible elements formally knit together—then it is philosophy that judges what the other two have given to it according to an act of free, comprehensive, and reflective valuation. The resultant creation is what Friedrich Nietzsche called a table of values, but one in which the values are related to one another according to an intellectual order.

The definitions presented above and their suggested order of relation are meant to be stipulative or, better, to reside in a zone between stipulative and essential definitions that cannot itself be precisely defined. They are not generalizations based on a survey of the meanings given to philosophy, religious experience, and psychology in the past, nor are they intended to describe the core of a great tradition or the termini of a rational process of historical development. These definitions are efforts to reorient philosophy and, therefore, to redefine it in a fresh way, but also in a way that remains relevant to the past, so that it can appeal to the past for some of its sustenance and inspiration. Philosophy, defined as the free, comprehensive, and reflective valuation of individuated life by a conscious center of such life, suggests a task that can be affirmed in the present historical period, which has charged the natural sciences with matters of explanation and causation, though not the interpretation of what those concepts mean. The task of evaluating personal experience has been practiced more by those generally called philosophers than by other kinds of thinkers, which means that their work provides the present inquiry with a usable past. Yet it would be unfair to past thinkers to say merely that they are useful for the present inquiry, even in a great measure—as they are. Inasmuch as it was through study of past philosophers, particularly the works of George Santayana, Alfred North Whitehead, John Dewey, Samuel Alexander, José Vasconcelos, Henri Bergson, and Antonio Caso, that the project of evaluation undertaken here became determinate, it is not surprising that aspects of their thought constitute that project or at least provide it with its basic patterns of reasoning.

The possibility for carrying out a free, comprehensive, and reflective valuation of personal life is rooted in a specific human experience in which the singularity of human life is made most vividly manifest. The experience in light of which one philosophizes is that which José Ortega y Gasset designated by the affirmation, "My life is the radical reality." The assumption of one's sovereignty over one's own life, which is inseparable from the declaration of that sovereignty—perhaps the only case in human experience in which words directly constitute a reality by drawing it out of an inchoate state of being—is the act of liberating one's judgment from submission to any external authority and, therefore, that of actualizing freedom. By feeling that one stands above one's life—in the sense of not feeling compelled to lose oneself in any one of life's partial pursuits, but is still oriented toward it in the sense that the self feels delivered to it as both its inescapable and proper object—one is enabled to achieve sufficient detachment to perform an evaluation of its partial pursuits.

The freedom released by assuming sovereignty over one's own life may touch the limit described in different ways by Albert Camus and Jean-Paul Sartre—at which the self is in suspense before the array of its possibilities, each of which flash into its awareness in a whirl of succession, but none of which claims its allegiance; a state not necessarily of dispassionate observation, but sometimes of alternating horror and joy, as each image makes its emotional impact but does not call out an active affirmation from the self. In contrast, freedom may also appear as a momentary burst of self-awareness immediately preceding a full deliverance of the self to a particular pursuit, either because the solicitation of that possibility is experienced by the self as appropriate to its participation in it or because that pursuit compels the emotions to such a degree that the self is swept away, often reluctantly and regretfully, into its actualization. The temper or tone of freedom required for philosophical inquiry falls between the extreme detachment of the suspended ego, which feels itself distinct from what it acknowledges to be its own life, and the fully committed ego, which nearly loses its distinction from the momentary experience in which it has become involved. The freedom constitutive of philosophy is neither indeterminate nor on the verge of decision, but is on the way to making a judgment, seeking experiences to review and criteria by which to evaluate their importance, and intermittently registering provisional judgments within the broader activity of search.

The assumption of sovereignty over one's own life—to which

Ortega's declaration that my life is the radical reality refers—
should not be understood as a means by which the self flees from
objectivity into a self-delusive solipsism. As Ortega put it, affirming the radical reality of my life does not mean that my life
is the only reality, but that it is the context in which all other
realities are rooted for me, specifically the things and persons I
acknowledge to be but that and who are, within that acknowledgment, held to be other than myself, though they enter into
my life. My life is open to and includes that which is not myself,
but is also that to which my self refers and which provokes it to
and evokes from it a concrete and relatively appropriate response. Yet although it is open to other realities, my life also is
separate—most conspicuously so when I declare my sovereignty
over it—and, indeed, cut off from any other reality. The self has
its own experience, which, in Ortega's terms, is intransferable
and insubstitutable. That experience is also finite, not only in
the sense that each of its moments begins and ends (past and
future are references from a finite present), but in the sense that
the individual's life as a whole is bounded by the abysses of
birth and death. The freedom released by the assumption of
sovereignty over my life is complemented by the sense of being
confined within it, of being incarcerated within the boundaries
of my skin and of the moments which, as John Locke observed,
perpetually perish.

The act of free valuation undertaken in philosophy proceeds
from a finite center of experience that is capable of comprehending both itself as a specific being and beings other than
itself. How union with *and* separation from that which is other
than myself can be jointly present in my life is not a concern for
philosophy as it has been defined here. A *direct* realism, such as
that set forth by Alexander, tends to emphasize union by making conscious experience a component of a wider knowing, perceiving, or sensing situation; whereas a *critical* realism, such as
Santayana's, tends to cut off the conscious center's world of

experience from other existents and ends by making existence
itself a postulate—albeit a spontaneous and unavoidable one—
of animal faith. Both the insight of direct realism and that of
critical realism are integral to understanding what the declaration of my life as the radical reality means, but neither is capable
of being reconciled in a self-consistent concept that includes
them both. The fact that my life is open to that which differs
from myself makes communicable and even public that act of
free valuation that is definitive of philosophy, whereas the clo-
sure of my life, its intimacy, makes that act personal and unique.

The act of self-possession—through which the freedom required
by philosophical inquiry is released—is not sufficient to constitute philosophy. One may stand above the momentary contents
of one's life and entertain possibilities relevant to them, finally
making a judgment about the import of those particular contents and possibilities, and then, most often, behaving in ac-
cordance with that judgment. The practical viewpoint, a sketch
of which has just been given, is always partial and, thus, in
Ortega's terms intra-vital. The moment of freedom is here a
phase of a wider activity, which has a functional relation to other
phases. It occurs when, as Dewey says, the human being meets
an obstacle to the unhampered expression of life and seeks to
restore ease of activity. That obstacle may be either external or
internal to the organism or the psyche, but in all cases possibilities are entertained to find a way to surmount frustration.
Similarly, freedom of mind may be applied to dwelling within
the products of imagination, either spontaneous daydreams or
ritualized fantasies, each of which is a particular content that
may be juxtaposed to others. Neither the practical, which includes the experimental sciences, nor the aesthetic mode of personal existence can be liberated from subservience to parts.
Even the most general sciences proceed from specific observations of certain facts, and even the most profound works of art

have a specific tone, project particular images, and often utilize symbolism derived from certain concrete events. Practical and aesthetic life determine freedom with regard to particular contents. This does not mean they should be denigrated, but only, for present purposes, that they should not be confused with philosophy.

Philosophical inquiry, which itself becomes determinate in an evaluation of life, has a special relation to freedom that is expressed by an interest in comprehensiveness. To evaluate personal life adequately, philosophical activity must strive to observe that life as a whole, standing above not only practical and aesthetic modes of life, but also above the more inchoate experiences of distraction, panic, dreaming, and—so far as it can draw it toward awareness—dreamless sleep. The kind of comprehensiveness sought by philosophy is not awareness or com-prehension of an aggregate of particulars, nor of whatever general laws of relation characterize the succession of groups of particulars or their characteristics. Rather it is attention to the full range of experiences that are significant in forming and orienting personal existence. There is a necessary circularity involved in the discussion of comprehensiveness so long as it does not mean a grasp of everything that is. In the present case philosophical inquiry is guided by a quest for comprehensiveness about that which is significant. Yet significance or importance is just what is to be determined by a free, comprehensive, and reflective valuation, which means that comprehensiveness cannot be abstracted fully from a prior or concurrent judgment about content or substance. Comprehensiveness is a way of determining freedom of mind in the least possible degree; but it does not avoid giving philosophical activity a particular vital tone, which is one of concern for what is significant (if not always what is serious), and vigilance against either an indiscriminate embrace of all of life's contents or a single-minded devotion to one or a few of them. Comprehensiveness requires a disposition to be alert to new orders of significance and also a sense for the whole, held without any assurance that a definition of it is adequate.

Both the freedom and the comprehensiveness of the judgment at which philosophy aims contain the characteristic of reflexivity, which is included in the definition of philosophical inquiry as a separate term because it functions to unify the other two. Reflexivity refers to the form of self-consciousness or self-awareness involved in assuming sovereignty over one's life in an act of self-possession which allows distance of the self from any of life's particular contents, and the consequent recognition of the self by itself as separate from and related to life's contents. Reflexivity is most intense and highly developed in the quest for comprehensiveness, which demands that the self be identified with its life, in the sense of struggling to grasp it as a whole, but discriminated from it—in the sense of holding it open to judgment. Reflexivity is acute in the tension between the zero point of pure indifference, at which the self reposes back upon itself and glides from one experience to the next, and the absorption of the self into one of the contents of its life. Wandering above life in a detached manner delivers the self to an experience in which each content is taken simply as a possibility that is, in Santayana's terms, intuited as an essence; whereas plunging into the vital flow fuses the self with actuality so that its distinctness is lost. Reflexivity is furthered by the quest for comprehensiveness because comprehensiveness requires that when one scrutinizes any form of experience one should be aware of other kinds of experience that limit its range of application. In a most elementary sense, for example, the effort to understand and evaluate experiences of pleasure should be undertaken in awareness of experiences of pain, boredom, and frustration, among others. Reflexivity makes such a comparative review possible and is stimulated by that review.

In philosophical activity, the destiny of freedom, comprehensiveness, and reflexivity is evaluation, a term used here synonymously with valuation, so long as valuation is understood to be conscious. The fundamental way in which life and its contents are evaluated is in terms of their significance or importance, as Alfred North Whitehead pointed out in *Modes of Thought*. Whitehead, indeed, dignified importance to the extent that an integral aspect of his cosmology is a god, part of the nature of which is to value all possibilities in an eternal act of envisagement according to their significance. The thought presented here does not rely upon such concepts as "god," "eternity," or "envisagement" to secure whatever unity it achieves, but leaves the act of valuation to the individual philosopher, which means that the ideas of "importance" and "significance," which demand a point of reference, are relative to each philosopher's judgment. The preceding discussion has indicated, however, that the relativity of philosophical activity and its products to the individuals who create those products does not signify a descent into the kind of subjectivity associated with whim or an abandonment of constructive thought in favor of an inquiry into the conditions—whether biological, social, cultural, or psychological—under which certain forms or contents of thought arise at particular places and times. Significance and importance are terms pointing to the way in which the contents of life enter into philosophical activity; they are the most general concepts available for designating that which evaluation expresses, from the standpoint of its receptivity, and establishes, from the viewpoint of its constructivity. Evaluation in terms of importance becomes philosophical when it strives to achieve freedom, comprehensiveness, and reflexivity.

The radical reality of individuated life, which it is the task of philosophy to evaluate freely, comprehensively, and reflexively, reveals itself through experience. Those experiences concerned with the rooted realities that occur within personal existence provide philosophy with the material on which it works to create tables of values; but they do not provide it with a sense of life itself, both in emotional and cognitive terms. That total sense of life is available in certain of what traditionally have been called religious experiences. Whitehead laid hold of the special character of some religious experiences when he related religion to the "subjective response" of the person to the cosmos. The person's response to life as a whole does not refer here to any reflective valuation of life, which is also a personal response, but to a complex of feelings out of which certain judgments spontaneously arise. Those judgments carry the certitude with them of what John Henry Newman called "real assents," as opposed to "nominal assents," which are judgments accepted because they are convenient, widespread in society, or fill gaps between judgments more firmly rooted in concrete experience. There is a primal experience of what life is that is prereflective and that provides the content that religions symbolize and that theologians systematize on the ground of religious symbolism. Much religion may be understood, indeed, as an effort to reconcile human beings to the disquieting contents and judgments that define the primal experience of life. Theology may enter as a project of rationalizing some religious reconciliation or as a critique—which is undertaken to draw the individual back to the religious symbolism—of any such effort at rationalization. There is also a "natural theology" which attempts to perform the task of reconciliation through metaphysics, as evidenced by the classical modern thinkers from René Descartes to Whitehead. As much as do religions and the theologies associated with them, such natural theology depends on the primal experience of life. Philosophy as defined here is not theological but dwells within the primal experience of life and absorbs its emotions, thereby gaining a basis of content for its judgments of importance.

What is called here the primal experience of life was described by Rudolf Otto, in terms of "the idea of the holy," as that

of the *mysterium tremendum et fascinans,* and by Edgar Allen
Poe as the sense of "awe." There is no way to describe this
experience in strictly self-consistent terms because it combines
in a single feeling disharmonious emotions and opposing vital
dispositions. The idea of a terror that attracts points to the matrix
out of which arise contrasting and partial judgments, such as
those which ground optimism and pessimism. But those judgments are not able to do justice to the experience of terror.
In times of what Nietzsche called "declining life," the person
tends to recoil from life itself, overwhelmed by its destructive
force; whereas in periods of ascension erotic tendencies toward
union guide the self, which feels that nature as a whole is
favorable to it. There are, however, brief moments at which the
person is neither in flight from life, either attempting to tyran-
nize over it or to withdraw from it, nor in league with it, but
is captured by its full duality. The awe that suffuses and is expressed in the experience of the *mysterium tremendum et
fascinans* suspends any release of the self into overt activity and,
as Otto asserts, is the basis for worship, which does not intervene
to transform its object. However, when worship occurs within
the context of a religion that reconciles the duality of terror and
attraction in favor of the attractive, it tends to become prayer—
which begins with thanksgiving but leads almost imperceptibly
to petition and then, sometimes, on to conjuring, which is the
effort to intervene when intervention is impossible. Worship itself already signals a reconciliation of the self with the duality
of life and nature, which is consubstantial with life but is felt
to be also opposed to it—though influential, if not determinative, over it. The awe upon which worship may be engrafted is
not worshipful itself because it does not make the *mysterium
tremendum et fascinans* an object but is seized by it as the very
feeling of what life is most completely, though not in a norma-
tive sense what it is in its "fullness."

When undertaken critically, attempts of conceptual thought

to articulate precisely what the experience of awe means, end in
concepts that lack coherent content because they refer to opposing terms. The most concise and critical expression of the constructive theologian's interpretation of the idea of the holy was
provided by Nicholas of Cusa who characterized divine reality as
a *coincidentia oppositorum*. Short of metaphysics the import of
the experience of awe is best conveyed by the descriptions of
nature from the person's viewpoint that are provided by such
naturalists as Samuel Alexander and George Santayana. Alexander spoke of "nature that nurtures and destroys us," and
Santayana claimed that the human being judged the world
primordially by dividing it into "dominations" that threatened
its life, and "powers" that were beneficial to it. The destructive
tendencies in nature, its dominations, are encompassed in the
fearful component of awe, whereas its nurturant tendencies, its
powers, are contained in the reverential element of awe: the
mysterium tremendum et fascinans may be understood apart
from religious symbolism and from the efforts of theologians to
rationalize that symbolism as the sense that most adequately
grasps personal existence as a whole rather than in any of its
partial aspects.

The base of religious experience or vision of life on which
philosophy reposes may be further elucidated by appeal to the
Bhagavad-Gita. In that work, which recounts a conversation
between Krsna and the warrior Arjuna—who must be convinced
to go into battle against some of his friends and relatives, and,
thereby, to perform his social duty—Krsna normally appears in
the guise of a beautiful and good individual, the *fascinans*. But
at one point, Krsna suddenly decides to reveal himself to Arjuna
as the "universal vision," that all-inclusive combination of good
and evil, the *tremendum*. Arjuna gazes momentarily at the universal vision, which Krsna claims has never been vouchsafed to
any human being before, and then recoils from it and appeals
to Krsna to turn himself back into his benign countenance. The

lesson here is that human beings, even the most select among them—as Arjuna is—are incapable of living in light of the truth of reality, and that in order to conduct their lives at all, must view reality as favorable to them. It appears as if Krsna revealed the universal vision to humble Arjuna and make him realize that his misgivings about performing his duty could not be sustained because they were not based upon an adequate understanding of being. Krsna's judgment was determinative because it was based on tolerance of the universal vision. From the standpoint of individuated human life, which is conscious of its own life as the radical reality, the universal vision is approached in feeling by the experience of awe, and in intellect by the quest for comprehensiveness. Philosophy, as understood here, gains its characteristic mood from the duality expressed by Otto's *mysterium tremendum et fascinans,* and, therefore, dares to attempt what in the *Bhagavad-Gita* is thought to be at least imprudent, if not impossible and self-destructive.

The context in which synoptic vision occurs, as was stated at the outset of the present discussion, is illuminated by psychology, the project of describing precisely the structure of experience as it is known to the inward gaze of an individual human self. Psychology views the primal experience of life, that of the *mysterium tremendum et fascinans,* as an experience that belongs to the persons who have it and that shares a certain form with other experiences. In addition, the primal experience of life is knit together with other experiences in what is ordinarily known as an individual's life, which spans a number of moments. It is also psychology's business to describe how those moments are related to one another in a set of structures. Psychology in the sense meant here presumes the viewpoint of life grasped from within a body by a particular organism or self, that is, the life of a finite individual. Through the inward gaze the self opens out to its own life as it is experienced concretely without being referred beyond itself to any future destiny, whether it be some form of personal salvation, contribution through works to some future lives, or participation in a cycle of death and rebirth; or to an omnipresent reality, eternity. The field of individuated life is disclosed by assuming sovereignty over one's life, which constitutes philosophy as free inquiry, and it is also the domain of psychological description and the context in which the primal experience of life is interpreted.

The method of psychology is what Alexander called "simple inspection" of experience undertaken to describe the more pervasive forms and structures of that experience. "Simple inspection" presupposes that personal existence can be studied from within, can be objectified sufficiently to be scrutinized and described. It is on this point of objectification that the project of describing the life of a self from within is not susceptible to coherent exposition. How can the self get above itself or outside itself to inspect and describe itself? It cannot, because spatial imagery, though it seems to be unavoidable in stating any response to the question, is inappropriate in such a response. In justifying the method of simple inspection, Samuel Alexander argued that the act of inspecting itself could not be contemplated as an object, but that it was an "enjoyment" that included awareness of itself within its act of contemplating something else. His formula for conscious acts of mind with a cognitive import was, "I enjoy myself contemplating an object." Simple inspection requires that one be able to experience ("enjoy") oneself contemplating one's own responses, the responses of what may be called the "psyche" or "substantive ego" to that which impinges upon it and affects it, including the products of its own imagination and thought. Evidence that such a feat is possible is provided in everyday practical life in those experiences in which one "catches oneself" in a certain activity or mood. In the moment of "catching" one is aware of one's response to a situation, of that situation itself, and of the "catch."

The experience of "catching oneself" seems, indeed, to be the ground of more elaborate forms of self-understanding, such as simple inspection or, in the moral domain, what Gabriel Marcel calls "secondary reflection."

The description of the forms and structures of the experience of the finite self by itself from within is not undertaken from a position devoid of emotional and volitional content. Instead it is carried out within a specific attitude, albeit one that Alexander said is guided by the aim of restricting attention to what is "borne upon the face of what is being examined." Alexander described the appropriate attitude of the descriptive psychologist in the two suggestive oxymorons "deliberate innocence" and "strenuous naiveté." The pure psychologist, for Alexander, should attempt to look freshly at what appears to conscious mind by trying not to anticipate what will be found there and not to force ulterior relations on what is grasped by the inspection. "Deliberate innocence" and "strenuous naiveté" connote an effort to suspend judgment on the import of experience for the practical interests of the self, including within the notion of practicality the concern for survival after death (what Miguel de Unamuno called "transcendental economy") or for a purpose for one's life beyond living it well. It was such an attitude of "deliberate innocence" that guided the previous discussion of the primal experience of life as a *mysterium tremendum et fascinans,* and that informs the discussion in the second half of the present chapter, which is devoted to describing the forms and structures of personal existence through which values are evinced.

Before proceeding to descriptive psychology, it is only fair to drop briefly the mask of the relatively impersonal style in which the greater part of this book is written and to offer a personal statement of belief about the significance of life, so that my stance will be as obvious to a reader as it would be to someone

speaking to me face-to-face, which, of course, is not necessarily
so obvious. I am smiling right now and this book is written in
a smiling disposition. I have found in my past experience of
writing books that each one is written within the environment
of a determining mood, the search for and refinement of which
is what makes the book possible at all. Here, I think, I am just
proving to myself the wisdom of Martin Heidegger's suggestion
that our relation to the world is mediated by mood, which is
an attunement to being that is unanalyzable into abstract components. Philosophy as a free, comprehensive, and reflective
valuation of personal existence may be said to express what is
revealed to the conscious self about its own life through the
light cast by the mood in which it works. Indeed, it is precisely
because of how important mood is in determining what
philosophy expresses that philosophy is valuation. Mood is
selective: it is, at least, either good, bad, or agonizingly ambivalent, and its vicissitudes are probably closely related to the
level and direction of psycho-organic vitality—that is, whether,
in Nietzsche's terms, life is advancing or declining. If mood is
selective and if it enters directly into the content of philosophy,
then philosophy is selective and cannot be fully comprehensive.
I accept this conclusion gladly, adding only that I shall attempt
to seek comprehensiveness within my smiling mood by speaking
of ideas that grew out of very different moods, particularly the
more frowning ones. One might ask how philosophy can be a
free valuation if it is made determinate by a mood. The mood in
which I write a book is not merely received, but is also chosen,
yet chosen for its appropriateness to the expression of what I
deem to be most true about life. But truths about life are at
least partly relative to moods. I cannot escape the circle I am in
and must finally shrug my shoulders and proceed; or is it that I
choose to shrug my shoulders? Does it matter at all? What does
matter to me is that readers understand that I am trying to
clear myself of any Platonism, by which I mean the idea that it

is possible for the self to contemplate anything other than in a field of sensations and feelings that are bound to a body. "Knower" and "field," as the *Bhagavad-Gita* puts it, or conscious self and body, are inseparable: the destiny of the mind is the body, and through it the world to which the body is connected and the other personal existences who obtrude into that world. What I call philosophy is not undertaken for the purpose of constructing a philosopher's kingdom in which the self can dwell in order to find respite from the offenses and sometimes from the ecstasies of carnal existence, but as a training program for the task of living in truth and in goodness.

But I have strayed a bit from my initial purpose. I wanted to elaborate on the smiling mood. My smile is not the one with which Santayana said he wrote *Scepticism and Animal Faith,* that is, an ironical smile that proceeds from a reflective acceptance of and resignation to the limitations of existence. I do agree generally with Santayana that the only cure for birth and death is to enjoy the interval, but he seemed to apply that piece of wisdom in an effort to stand above that interval and grasp each event within it as a benevolent yet detached observer. I intend no criticism of Santayana by dissociating myself from his kind of smile; he taught me, after all, how to philosophize in good humor. I am just contrasting my character to his, and mine is one that operates by drenching itself in experiences and trying to absorb anything that is vitalizing from them. Having a basically reflective temperament I wish to preserve my detachment from each passing content of life but to minimize that detachment stringently in every experience that promises to advance life, in Nietzsche's sense, and not always my own life. I sometimes even have a taste for Dionysian ecstasy, for a kind of extravagance that through excess of enthusiasm loses a sense of proportion as a result of embracing the thrill of a particular moment. Philosophy, however, is about as Apollonian a practice as can be conceived of, and I intend to bring that characteristic of it to prominence by basing it substantively on a descriptive psychology of the finite self and on a dualistic vision of life (*mysterium tremendum et fascinans*). My smile is not ironical, but it also is not what I might call the "cosmic laugh," which is released in the moment of ecstasy when the self feels that it is more than just a finite human being and has somehow been empowered to override at will the vetoes on exuberance set up by more cautious souls partly to protect themselves from themselves and partly to protect themselves from others. My smile is infused by a bubbling up of cosmic laughter, but also by a sense of final despair, which is my analogue to Santayana's ironical detachment. The despair over finitude and the pricks of its messengers, disease and decay, are, indeed, more fundamental in determining my mood than is the joyous laughter at the spectacle of existence, which some Hindus think of as a holy game. Life is a holy game and if one is fortunately endowed, I think it can be played with competence and *élan*. But we are eventually losers, and after years of trying to absorb the wisdom of resignation I am still unreconciled to the defeat, though its inevitability becomes ever clearer.

The oxymoron that appropriately describes the mood in which I am writing this book is vivacious despair; I wish to emphasize that despair is the substantive and vivacity the qualifier. I have suffered, of course, morbid despair, but it so saps the will to live that no writing can be done under its influence. If vivacity cannot be maintained in the face of the continual affronts each of us suffers from ourselves, our bodies, our external environment, and other selves, then our alternatives are morbid despair, which precipitates a decline toward suicide, or one of the many forms of desperation, ranging from homicidal mania to sacrificial depression, the latter of which is often glorified, through the dynamic that Nietzsche called *ressentiment,* as faith. Just as I abhor the thought of withdrawing into a philosopher's kingdom of intellectual ideas, I am also re-

pelled by a faith in any unfulfilled promise. Instead of gaining
the will to survive by seeing my actual and concrete life in terms
of a future life promised to me, and then only if I fulfill certain
conditions, I pit the inner resources of my body, psyche, and
conscious self, and the "powers" in the world around me, against
the "dominations" from without and within. And I do it as long
as my resources are not exhausted. An excess of vivacity, when
it can be channeled into the description and evaluation of experience (descriptive psychology and philosophy) sometimes
issues forth into written expression. In my case, the very fact
that such expression is undertaken bespeaks a deeper affirmation
of life as the ground of the sustaining mood of vivacious despair.
My philosophy would be at odds with myself were it to express
a vision that detracted from life rather than one that defended
it against its despisers. I will not shrink from defending life
explicitly now and then, but I will mostly describe personal
existence as precisely as I can, trying to show it for what it is
when hope for significance beyond it is removed, putting in as
intelligible order as I can those things that I find make it good.
My aim is to defend life by describing what can be good about
it, always keeping in mind its utter misfortune and the evils
attendant on that misfortune.

Existence, as it is known to us primordially, is personal in the
sense of belonging to a self. The relation between self—a reality
that fluctuates between the poles of purely observant ego and
substantial mind, or psyche—and its internal and external environment is the only one to which the term "belonging"
properly applies, or at least applies in its fullest sense. In an
external sense, when aspects of the environment are being compared and contrasted, to belong means merely to form part of
something else. Each part stands alongside the others and in
such case the whole cannot be said to be greater than its parts.
The relation of self to its environs is not one of juxtaposition but

of comprehension. The self, as manifest in the declaration-proposition "my life is the radical reality," englobes its existence and stands at the center of it, judging it. That owned life or personal existence is, as Ortega noted, inalienable, insubstitutable, and intransferable: the life of a self belongs to it so intimately that it cannot even be taken as an object of thought and compared to others of its type. When people speculate about what it would be like to be someone else, that imagination itself arises as an aspect of their own lives. In addition it is always themselves that they imagine as another person; they do not become different selves with new lives. One can never be sure that one's experience shares the same sort of quality as someone else's, and that the inference of similarity is not based simply on fortuitous coordination or on some natural processes that have not been or cannot be understood. Yet the very inquiry undertaken here, descriptive psychology, depends upon the intention to treat my own experience as though it were, in its general characteristics, similar to that of others or, perhaps, representative of or even paradigmatic of others' experience. That "as if" is not merely a gratuitous or an expedient resort but a conviction that informs my own life on most waking occasions with the steadiness of one of John Henry Newman's "real assents." There are, however, the other occasions, those when personal existence reveals most completely its personal character, in which insight into the uniqueness and singularity of one's experience engenders lived doubt, as C. S. Peirce called it, about its ability to represent that of others. Those relatively rare occasions—when one grasps one's uniqueness—can be cultivated by contemplation on what they reveal and make it necessary for a descriptive psychology that is self-reflexive to be an invitation to others to see if they find an account to be adequate to themselves, and not a statement of universal principles.

At its most vivid level the grasp of one's existence as personal leads to the judgment that one is radically separated from all that which is other than oneself. One may, for example, wake up on a summer morning, walk outside and look at the sunrise, and feel that beyond the bounds of one's perceptual field there is nothing at all, just an indescribable emptiness that might be symbolized by the black border on some postage stamps honoring the dead. Radical separation may be accompanied by feelings of loneliness, in case the self experiencing it desires to be in communion with others, or by feelings of solitude, when the self is at ease alone. Whatever feelings characterize it, however, radical separation is a state that fixes limits and discloses finitude. It should not be confused with solipsism, the idea that the self is the all-in-all, the unique reality. Even at the points at which personal existence is etched against a background of nothingness, it is felt to be cut off, restricted, bounded—that is, only itself and nothing else. If the sense of radical separation begins to inform the momentary experiences (what Whitehead called the occasions) of personal existence, it deepens into an awareness of one's being-toward-death and then on into an appreciation of the particularity of one's environment, bodily states, moods, mentality, and even thought. The appreciation of one's limits— negatively through insight into the centricity of one's self, and positively through one's acknowledgment of one's specificity— shows up what is other to the self in the light of what Josiah Royce termed "contrast effects." Indeed, when the other is nothingness the contrast effects are the most stark and brilliant of all.

The state of radical separation is the seedbed in which mature those dispositions toward existence that existentialists have stressed, such as anxiety, nausea, and despair. When one cultivates radical separation one is continually brought back to one's limits, particularly to the finitude of personal existence, the death that lies somewhere ahead, and to the harbingers of that death—such adverse elements of life as disease and decay. Confinement to one's own life—which is the sorrow that must

be borne in order to attain to the freedom of judgment that constitutes philosophy—can breed a sense of frustration that fosters
rage against one's own debility and against the brutality of the
environment, then to a restless desperation that cannot be
solaced, and at last to a chronic hatred of existence that fosters
tendencies to destroy others or oneself. By learning to tolerate
adversity and to enjoy beneficence, one recovers from the hatred
of existence, which is not a particular animus directed against an
aspect of the self or of the environment, but a revulsion against
personal existence as a whole. When the hatred of existence is
acute, however, the attitude of the self is one of intolerance, of
rebellion doomed to frustration from the outset because it is
rebellion against oneself, which can only destroy the self. Yet
personal existence is such that when it declares itself to be what
it is by acknowledging what it is, it becomes, as Heidegger noted,
concerned for itself. Most often that concern is not expressed as
the resolute determination to fulfill a self-authorized project,
but as acute awareness of the vulnerability of the self to danger
(what the American existentialist David Swenson called "objective insecurity"), and to collapse (its inability to maintain
sufficient morale to sustain itself at a steady or ascending level
of vitality and interest in its environment). When such concern
cannot be satisfied, because the awareness of fragility and vulnerability has become too sharp, the self may vainly try, as
Dewey observed, to "get outside itself" by inserting itself into
a greater whole, constructed of symbols: radical insecurity finds
compensation in the "quest for certainty." If such efforts are not
effective or fail, the alternatives are either to sink into bitterness
and cultivate, gradually or abruptly, one's death, or to tolerate
the revulsion against life, which should not be suppressed altogether because it is a primal response of personal existence to
itself.

Personal existence, though radically separate from what is not
itself, is composed of a relation between self and what environs

it. That relation is mediated by the body or organism, which is both an aspect of the self's environment and an integral component of the self. The personal existent considered most concretely is what Miguel de Unamuno called the *hombre de carne y hueso,* the man of flesh and bone, who "is born, suffers, and dies." In the state of radical separation the body is felt to be intrinsic to the self though often subversive of its desires. The body gives the rest of the environment to the self and shapes it, more or less effectively, for the self. It is through the body that the self becomes most directly aware of its limits. Close inspection of the experience of the body shows it to be in the main spontaneous and not subject to deliberate control. The body, indeed, fundamentally "lives" the self rather than being "lived" by it, yet when existence is self-consciously personal, the self over-looks the body. That over-looking reveals that the body is a death trap, an imperfectly construed set of organs and functions vulnerable to accident and subject to degeneration. It is mutable and its changes touch the more substantial aspects of the mind— sensation, feeling, and mood—which call attention not only to their data but to what they reveal about the body's fragility. None of the foregoing remarks should be understood to involve deprecation of the perfections of the experience of the body such as pleasure, vitality, and coordination, all of which may be nurtured as finite goods under favorable conditions. The point is that such goods arise and are brought into being within a context of existence which, when it is fully acknowledged to be personal and not merely an element of a wider whole, is revealed to be boundlessly significant, indeed, precious, and also finite, a chamber of horrors. Paul of Tarsus, the first existentialist, exercised such recognition when he contrasted the dying and decaying "flesh" to the new body that would be granted to the blessed. Personal existence as it is defined here discloses when it is lucid to itself a self that is cornered like a desperate animal in its own flesh and unable (in Dewey's terms) to get outside itself. From the standpoint of a life that is limited, dependent on an environment for its sustenance, and subject to termination, philosophy makes its judgments of significance.

Not only is the self enclosed in a life, a stretch of time from birth to death dotted by spans of attention revealing qualities and the mental expressions of and thoughts about them, but it is also encased, when it is self-aware, in some particular momentary experience. I concur with Alfred North Whitehead in finding the locus of being, the *res vera* or true thing, in an "actual occasion," a "drop of experience." I differ from Whitehead only in confining the actual occasion to a moment of conscious experience, the primary type of which is what Santayana called a present moment in which an essense is intuited. At the core of momentary experience is a present, the presence of which is obtrusive, crowding out prospection (anticipation of the future), retrospection (concern to recover the past), and extrospection (adapting oneself to the requirements of another self). The primal present, the nub of actuality, is what Samuel Alexander called a "simple inspection" of what appears. For Alexander, the conscious enjoyment of an experience was distinct from that which was enjoyed in it, a quality other than itself. The paradigmatic experience was, for him, that of the mere "compresence" or "juxtaposition" of a percept and an awareness or a perceiving of it.

Just now I looked out of a window and saw a dump truck roll by spreading sand on the pavement. My gaze at that truck took in a tract of time during which I perceived a moving-truck-spreading-sand; that is, I intuited one of Santayana's essences. That present moment had a beginning and an end, but between them it was unbroken, what mystics who know the perfection of the moment would think of as a slice of eternal life. My perceiving of the sand spreading was discriminated from the percept and was on the edge of becoming aware of that split.

As soon as self-awareness was achieved I began to cogitate
about the significance of the event for illuminating the structure
of experience, engaging mainly in retrospection, and tried to
keep the experience, by then already irretrievably past, vivid to
awareness. The experience itself did not beg to be interrogated
but simply occurred, was self-sufficient. Practitioners of Zen,
Sufism, and Hasidic Judaism attempt to make each momentary
experience of their lives its own excuse for being, something
that is enjoyed for its own sake and affirmed in and for its own
actuality. Whether or not such a project is pursued, the peace
that surrounds a moment of conscious experience—the momentary character of which is evident—is compelling for a restless
psyche.

Surrounding the core of actuality, which is the intuition of an
essence, is a wider yet less precise domain of actuality which may
be called the "lived present." The lived present is the here-and-
now, the context in which the primary responses of the self to
its environment are occurring. It is in this context that the self
is concretely exhibited as a substantial ego in constant transaction
through its body with that which is other than itself. In the
lived present the self may be said to be standing in actuality, as
when I leave my writing to look up and gaze about or hear
scraps of conversation. I am aware of myself, not as a thinking
ego, but as a man of flesh and bone who is perceiving a world
of qualities and commenting about it. I comprehend myself as
here at this table listening to these people. I am confident that if
I analyzed it, the moment in which I am participating would
turn out to be composed of numerous spans of attention, each as
neatly framed as the intuition of sand spreading. These building
blocks, however, have already been passed over by an ego that
has become distanced from any one of them through its internal
discourse about them. The distance between ego and any of the
chunks of framed quality that emerge and pass away gives the
lived present imprecise boundaries; it is, as William James

noted, "fringed" by other experiences, which have just occurred
or are about to rise to awareness.

John Dewey's term "unstable individual" aptly describes the
here-and-now for a personal existent. In one respect the individual's spatiotemporal context of orientation is what is
maximally real, an anchor holding the self fast to the world. In
another sense it is as flimsy and fleeting as the spans of attention
that constitute it as presence, and that are unified by discourse.
A lived present defined by the act of observing, or what might
be called "framing the occasion," can give way abruptly to one
determined by response to a perceived threat or to the appearance of something desired or someone loved. Quick shifts of
attention are changes in context of orientation: perceptual space
narrows or widens in response to the interest guiding the self,
just as time "hangs heavy" or "flies" depending upon how congenial the self finds its context. The pure actuality of the intuition of essence contains no sense of a spatial beyond and no
apprehension of the passage of time, whereas the broader
actuality of the lived present encompasses both because it is
formed by a response of the self that binds frames of experience
around the expression of interests. Even at its most receptive the
lived present involves sufficient concentration to keep contemplation in effect. But the kinds of temporal passage and
spatial beyond are different in the context of here-and-now
than they are in ordinary practical thinking. Change occurs in
the lived present within a certain situation defined in terms of an
interest—for example, an activity such as driving to the store.
The past is the past of that drive, the future that which has not
yet been driven. Similarly, the beyond is the space traversed and
that not yet traversed. The lived present is formed of what
one might call vital space and time.

For ordinary practical thinking the past is a storehouse of
events ranged in an order of succession, and the future is a grid
of succession in which events will occur when due, whether or

not one believes they have been foreordained. Past and future here are defined in opposition to actuality, but for practical thinking this is not apparent; both dimensions are felt to be as real as the present. From the viewpoint of the self aware of the here-and-now, however, actuality may become so vivid that the self becomes cognizant of its life as a sporadic series of momentary experiences, each of which is exactly itself, and none of which has any necessary relevance for the current lived present. At such moments the present may either be embraced for its own sake or contrasted with that which is past, future, and other. In the latter case the self becomes enclosed in actuality in an analogous sense to which it is locked within its flesh. From an apprehension of vivid actuality the past is felt to have a quality of "pastness," which means that far from being a storehouse of potentially useful experience it is understood as the domain of what was once actual, but is now only retrievable through memory—which is grasped as a present experience directed toward the past or, better, referent to it. The actuality of the past event is judged to be irretrievable and, indeed, a nullity but for any effects that it might be prolonging into the present. When lovers part they are most lucid when they recognize that their last embrace was nothing more than a fine actuality, and that their next experience will be an actuality of being by themselves with a new context of orientation.

From the standpoint of a self-affirmed actuality the future is judged to be even more of a nullity than the past, which at least was actual. The "futurity" of the future is its character of not being yet, the "yet" signifying an assent to the belief that events will be. But that they will be for the self, which can meet with catastrophe at any moment, is always uncertain. In the present that obtrudes its presence there is a sense that the future is indefinite, so much so that the self has very little determination over it, indeed, that anything might happen. The sense of the pastness of the past engenders an intense nostalgia that is neutralized by the awareness of its futility, whereas the sense of the futurity of the future is a breeding ground of hopes that are dashed immediately by critical reflection.

Actuality is usually the privilege of a radically individuated self, not of a relation between or among selves, which involves most often anticipation and remembrance, and, thus, dwells in the medium of symbolic time. There are, however, exceptions, those experiences of communion in which persons have become so attuned to each other that they share not only common understandings, but also the emotional and valuative tenor of those understandings. At such moments the participant selves are transfixed on one another and their very union becomes, it seems, a jointly intuited essence, each drinking in the other's. Moments of communion are rare and fleeting, at least for the kinds of selves that have emerged in the modern West, but they are the best experiential grounds for the possibility of knowing other minds as self-referential (as minds) rather than as intelligible through their works. Most ordinary communication rests on an implicit faith that communion exists, that there is a sympathetic and responsive self with me to whom an appeal can be made to feel as I do and, thus, to judge as I do. With the spread of complex organizations, however, communication tends to be premised not on communion but on operational rules—whether legal or technical—that exclude feeling, emotion, and individual will. Were such abstract mediations among individuals to become pervasive, the experience of the other self as actual self might be greatly weakened or even lost, and society would be degraded to a collection of isolated centers of awareness sustained by an apparatus that included themselves as means to fulfilling collective projects or as mere repositories for production.

At the opposite pole from communion is the experience of being absolutely alienated from other selves in a situation, in the sense of being convinced that one would be incapable of achieving communion with them. There are times when a person who has become sensitive to the moods at play within a situation senses a radical disharmony among them and is thrown into a lonely isolation. Such disharmony is most often a result of the person's being gripped by terror at the marks of finitude while the others are occupied with being sociable, performing a task, or venting their resentments or *ressentiment.* The others in such case seem to the person to belong to another species, to lack, indeed, any depth, any interiority at all. Their faces take on a masklike appearance and they become unreachable. Unamuno opined in *The Tragic Sense of Life* that there would be much greater happiness in the world if people were to run out into the streets and share with each other their horror at dying. It is just that horror, of course, that ordinary social relations seek to suppress, both in order to get tasks accomplished and to prevent the very communion of sorrow Unamuno prescribed. Yet the sufferer from the sickness unto death wants more than anything else to share despair with other selves. The social compact, which most fundamentally is a conspiracy to uphold morale, seems to the sufferer to be a tissue of hypocrisy, and revulsion against it may become so intense that an infinite distance opens up between self and others; a kind of social death occurs. At such points the other persons are presenced to the self as wholly other.

The "otherness" of the other self is brought to light in the acknowledgment that the other is the center of a personal existence, someone whose own life is a radical reality. That acknowledgment may arise, as it so often does when the ego first becomes conscious of itself, through a betrayal of trust that the self had in its protectors. The child who has not yet become defiant feels its own individuality to be joined to other selves: the child is in the paradoxical position of regarding itself as an absolute center of existence that is at the same time a satellite of greater centers. At the moment of self-assertion against others this paradox is exploded and the self falls out of its orbit and seizes, at least for an instant, its absolute centricity, its personal existence. Yet, having fallen out of orbit, the child has no direction of its own and is still dependent on the care and protection of others for its survival. Its assertion of individuality tends to be destructive, often culminating in the introjection of aggression, which takes such forms as thoughts of how much the protectors would suffer if the child were injured or killed. Under the foregoing interpretation, delusional psychosis would be traced to an adaptation by the child to a situation in which those upon whom it is dependent for sustenance and protection are unreliable and, indeed, are threats. Autism would be a pure assertion of individuality by way of negation of the others. It is the direction of all childhood rebellion and the point toward which all regression in later life tends.

Once the other has been revealed as other to the self, a susceptibility grows to acknowledging one's experienced world as one's own and no one else's. It may become clear to the person that whatever hatred of existence is felt by the self belongs to it alone and cannot be dispelled by sharing but can either be kept under control or spread by contagion. At that point the person recognizes that the sickness unto death is alleviated only by a private struggle and not by communion, which is one of the most precious finite goods, but an especially fleeting one. The self that reaches such a judgment on its condition is prepared to enjoy solitude, which is the affirmed state of being self-consciously apart from others and with oneself by oneself. It is in solitude, not in dialogue, that the modern philosopher thinks and makes judgments about life. Solitude sets the self free and is especially conducive to the discrimination of an overseeing ego from a substantial ego, or psyche. The affirmation of being apart has no taint of loneliness, which is the condition of a self unwillingly cut off from communion with others. For the lonely person the other is other as an unattained object of desire and, thus, as a source of frustration. Loneliness is almost always bitter, because frustration breeds a sense of being aggrieved and finally a hatred for those who are still desired nonetheless. One who cultivates solitude is aware of the otherness of the other as a tragic failure of existence that provides the very freedom that crowns it.

Within a momentary experience the self exercises the two possibilities of being drawn out into the environment and of being drawn into itself. Ortega called these two directions of consciousness, respectively, *alteración* (otherhood) and *ensimismamiento* (in-oneselfness). They are similar to Jung's extraversion and intraversion, and point to the essential referential aspect of the self. Ordinary personal existence is extraverted, in the sense of being delivered over to a particular activity, what Ortega termed an "occupation." Such an "occupation" may be anything from withdrawing from a source of pain (nearly a reflex) to crafting a sentence while writing an essay (hyperreflexive), but it always involves the self becoming absorbed in the objects for which and on which it is working, the first serving to guide judgment on the transformations of the second, and in the performance. When consciousness is drawn out into the object most purely—that is, when transformative activity is directed only to making the body fit to deliver essences to a contemplative ego—Santayana's "intuition of essence" is achieved. Short of intuition of essence *alteración* involves being absorbed in each phase of an activity, keeping a sense, not always conceptually clear, of the degree of success being achieved. The extraverted consciousness gets "lost" in what it is doing, sometimes becoming "absent-minded." Indeed, absent-mindedness is a state of personal consciousness that is not self-consciously conscious and, therefore, not aware of its personal character: it is an experiential support for Jean-Paul Sartre's thesis that there is a prereflective *cogito*. Absent-mindedness, in the above sense, is ubiquitous, and, while one is awake, characterizes the great stretches of time when the self is

not aware of itself as a personal existence and does not declare
itself and know itself to be the "radical reality." The self drawn
out into the other knows it has been conscious when it catches
itself having been absorbed in an activity by comprehending that
activity as conscious. At such a moment an "I" asserts itself as
overseer of the activity, enriching or, in Whitehead's terms,
raising the "grade" of the consciousness, but not creating it. Intuition of essence is a burst of awareness that usually precedes
instantaneously the affirmation of the self-conscious ego. The
negation of that ego is not absorption into practicality but what
William James called "panic fear," the breakdown of control
over one's responses in the face of frustration from without or
horror and revulsion from within.

The second direction of the self, the turn inward, being
within oneself, is not the same as introspection, which is
normally a way of getting lost in remembrance of and response
to the self's own past (one of the varieties of *alteración*), but
is a grasping of the inwardness of the self, the focusing of a
center of awareness on all that is not itself. As Ortega notes,
ensimismamiento gains its foothold in everyday life when the
self holds back from making an immediate response to a situation and starts considering what to do next. The experience of
deliberating about a decision divides the self between a substantial ego with shifting moods and changing judgments, and
a judicial ego that takes command over the disposition of activity.
In *alteración* there is often the trace of a judicial ego present,
just enough to monitor performance, but it is indistinct and
excentric, appearing as an adhesion to the concrete activity: it is
more of a function of the events making up the activity than an
organizer, determiner, and comprehender of them. The direction of *ensimismamiento,* however, is away from both the
practical concerns that often initiate it and the organizing and
determining that respond to those perplexities, and toward the
position of comprehending for its own sake. Far from encourag-
ing self-involvement, in-oneselfness leads to the experience of

being an observer, of framing an occasion with one's oversight of it. In the lived present the inward turn usually means being a detached observer of a situation and making judgments about it. Sometimes that detachment can become so precise that not only are the objects in the environment held at a distance from the self, but so are the judgments made upon them. At such a point the self observes itself responding to the solicitations of its environment. The highest pitch of detachment is similar to the intuition of essence, in that both are pure awareness of what is distinct from awareness. Framing an occasion to the degree that the substantial self, making particular judgments, is an aspect of the occasion, differs from mere intuition of essence by revealing a personal existence.

In both modes of self-direction—otherhood and in-oneself-ness—there is a discrimination between awareness and all that appears in its light. The awareness is least obtrusive in those experiences in which the self is absorbed in an activity, and most conspicuous when the self is overseeing itself and its environment. The distinction between awareness and what it comprehends is most clearly made in the Hindu tradition, particularly in the *Bhagavad-Gita,* where the discrimination of "knower" from "field" is said to be the "highest form of knowledge." In the *Gita* the "field" is interpreted primarily as the body, which is intermediate between the objects with which it comes in contact and the mentality for which it is provider of its rudimentary moods and the executor of its judgments. Pure awareness, without any content or object, and pure vitality, without any consciousness of it, are abstractions from the standpoint of momentary experience, but they are useful concepts for indicating that experience—as the Mexican philosopher José Vasconcelos taught—is a "coordination of heterogeneous elements." Whether these elements can or do exist by themselves is a matter for poetic speculation, though modern consciousness, influenced by the hypothesis of biological evolution to emphasize the importance of the body, tends to believe that life processes are mostly nonconscious, and that awareness cannot exist without the help of a properly construed body. From the perspective of the self-conscious ego grasping itself from within, neither evolutionary naturalism nor its interlocutor absolute idealism, which reverses the order of dependence affirmed by the former, is convincing. The tendency of the self overseeing and thereby grasping personal existence is to find the distinction between awareness and all of the various dynamized qualities that make up the contents of life to be so remarkable that the two elements of momentary experience are left separate from each other. Much of modern metaphysics may be interpreted as an effort to unite awareness and quality through some symbolic mediation such as "nature," "the absolute," or "neutral substance." There is, however, no need for such a mediation, except to make the self more comfortable with its existence, because momentary experience combines the two elements spontaneously. In its most rudimentary form the combination is what Samuel Alexander called sheer compresence, which is not felt to carry any causal priority or relation of dependence with it, but is not marked by any sense of disjunction or alienation. The sharp and precise discrimination of knower from field is, indeed, an achievement of concentration and of a life orderly and satisfied enough to have stretches of leisure in which the radical reality of personal existence becomes conspicuous. The *Gita* calls the distinction "the highest form of knowledge" because it is difficult to attain and definitive of personality—though it is present, albeit confusedly, in every momentary experience. Discrimination of knower from field is not a conceptual distinction, but a concrete experience, which not only clarifies the components of experience, but also restrains the substantial ego from discharging its primary responses to what it receives into overt activity or even into extravagant imagination.

Philosophy, as a free, comprehensive, and reflective valuation of life is given a general content by the sense of life—which is

made explicit by a vision of being to which the self responds—
and psychology, which describes the structures of conscious life.
In the present study the experience of life is understood as one of
the ambivalence of nature, the cognitive import of which is
expressed in Samuel Alexander's observation that nature "nurtures and destroys us." The experience of the *mysterium tremendum et fascinans* and the sharp contrast between ascending and
declining life generally evident throughout the range of experiences leads the self to make a fundamentally ambivalent response to its existence. Nurturance, which is expressed consciously as vivacity or zest for life, leads to an affirmation of
existence, a love of its dynamism, because the prospering organism moves freely and easily from one moment to the next.
Destruction, which appears consciously as suffering or distaste
for life, leads to a hatred, a denial of existence, whether projected outward on the world or other persons, or inward on the
self. Nihilism is intelligible in light of the destructive aspects of
nature. However much the self affirms life, there will come a
time when life is denied to it and, most often, before then a time
when it denies life. Only a will to believe can uphold a continuous affirmation of life in the face of its decadence, and such
a will wins out by deadening the very blood of conscious
existence, the stream of direct sensation. To be a lover and
partisan of life, not of faith or hope, it is necessary to affirm
existence in light of its duality and of the final victory of destruction for each personal existent. The following chapters will
show one way such an affirmation can be made: the way of
axiology, or the study of what makes life worthwhile.

Psychology here offers mainly two insights: that existence is
personal and that experience is momentary. Personal existence,
the character of which becomes most lucid to awareness in the
declaration-proposition "my life is the radical reality," is finite.
The act of possessing one's own existence brings with it recognition that there are other realities than oneself that are rooted in

one's life, some of which are destructive. Personal existence is most concretely described by the image of "the man of flesh and bone," who "is born, suffers, and dies." The personal existent is locked within a skin, upon which it depends for its inwardness, yet it is open to what is other than itself, which it appropriates and makes intimate, or attempts to reject. It is within the limits of personal existence that what is worthwhile appears: all value is for a self or selves. Similarly momentary experience is marked by finitude and limitation. From the bare intuition of essence, a prediscursive element of conscious experience, to the lived present that is marked by overseeing an occasion, actuality is conspicuous by its temporal and spatial restrictions. A cultivation of the vividness of actuality leads to a real and deep assent to the judgments that the past is no more and that the future is not yet: that the very locus of being, indeed, its seat, is a fleeting and flimsy momentary consciousness. Reflection on the experience of the other self also reveals limitation, in the sense that but for brief moments of communion personal existence is solitary; there is no access to the intimacy of the other and even orientation toward the other is clearly understood to be one's own. The fruit of psychology is the clear and lucid acknowledgment of the finitude of personal existence and of momentary experience. Values are for a self and are actualized within a moment.

What makes personal existence worthwhile, what is valuable in it and about it, will here be called virtue, and, so, what is offered in the following chapters is an account of the most general virtues, presented in an intelligible order of dependence, which when viewed as a totality is a description of "the good life." The term virtue is used here to epitomize goodness in order to stress what I consider to be the active character of the good, even when that activity is expressed, as it often is, by the intense concentration necessary to renounce, refrain, or forebear. Virtue also connotes an emphasis on the personal aspect of goodness, that goodness proceeds from and characterizes a self, that it is the achievement of a self constituted in part by the references it makes to itself, to objects within its environment, and to other selves. I do not apologize for using a term with such a masculine set of associations, the vital content of which is virility in the most general sense. Intrinsic to vivacity is what Nietzsche called the "feeling of power," which is developed by accustoming oneself to overcoming obstacles that proceed from the psyche, the body, the things in the world, and other selves. That glory in struggle and seeking of difficulty to work beyond it is a kind of virtue of virtues. Without it a person may achieve virtuous moments but not a good life. In the recent history of Western industrial societies women of the middle class have been taught to seek passive pleasures; they are far more likely to be found in mental hospitals than in prisons. Their liberation, which has not been achieved and is still a central task for contemporary society to fulfill, depends upon their learning to exercise virtue, particularly to hold their ground as individuals without caving into a would-be protector, whether well-intentioned colleague or aspiring tyrant (usually both). Much of the discussion to follow defends various self-disciplines and slights passive appreciation and being served by others, which is often the ideal of servants. The warrior's spirit of overcoming by going through the adversity of experience is appropriate to everyone, because everyone faces adversity. It should be particularly encouraged in women who need it more than anyone else in a competitive and indifferent society.

A virtue may be understood as a perfection of experience, there being three general virtues in correspondence with the three kinds of entities to which the self refers: itself, objects within the environment, and other selves. The perfection of the relation of the self to itself is self-control, which is composed of the three aspects of inward tolerance of the contents of life, including those that are destructive; the inward check upon the release of responses to life that spring from the hatred of existence; and acceptance by the self of its failures. To tolerate one's personal existence and accept one's failures one must know that existence as a whole, a task that is aided by combining the insights of psychoanalysis with the description of the salient features of waking experience. In order to exert an inner check upon one's expansive emotion one must cultivate practical self-discipline. Chapter II discusses self-control by interpreting the methods of psychoanalysis and practical self-discipline in terms of a description of the dynamics of the experience of self. The perfection of the relation of the self to objects in the world is artistry, that is, the enhancement of momentary experience through shaping its contents according to a design, what Samuel Alexander called forming an interpenetration of mind and material. Art is defined broadly here and includes the "fundamental arts" (those basic to living with some independence in contemporary society) such as cooking and driving; the reflective arts, such as fine art, science, statecraft, and philosophy; and the art of living itself, of bringing each momentary experience to its fulfillment. Chapter III provides an account of artistry, of the various kinds of art and their relation to each other. The relation of the self to other selves is perfected by love, which has the two aspects of forebearance—which allows the other to be free—and of concern, which serves the other and thereby creates the security out of which freedom emerges. The dialectic of love occupies Chapter IV. The virtues are ranged in an intelligible order of dependence, with self-control providing the basis for the effective practice of artistry, and the mastery of art giving a wisdom to love. In the other direction the virtues form an order of perfection, love fulfilling artistry by providing it with an appreciator and an appropriator, and artistry fulfilling self-control by giving it an occasion for concrete exercise. Each of the general virtues, however, is worthwhile in itself, its own excuse for being.

The self, that is, the personal existent, is a diversified unity that comprehends an individual life and is centered in an ego, a conscious "I" that grasps itself as the possessor of its life. It is not possible to define the self precisely, because it is the most inclusive term of all those relevant to the description of the general features of conscious life as understood from the viewpoint of a self-conscious grasp of that life from the inside (the formulation is unavoidably circular). At one margin the self is fused with the body and, indeed, with those aspects of the external world that are in contact with it and, by inference, even with objects beyond its ken. Here the self is what J. V. Bateman called a "me locus of reference" in mutual relations with that which is not itself. At the extreme the "me" is not sharply differentiated from that which is other than itself, and feels itself to be an integral component of a larger whole, though a qualitative whole and not one necessarily constituted by a meaning. At the other margin the self is contracted into a concentrated center of awareness, a focal point of consciousness that is barely personal and sometimes may be apprehended in some unaccountable way as an impersonal attention by that of which it is aware—which

itself is aware and personal—but continuous with what it appre-
hends. The foregoing account indicates experiences that can
only be described in contradictory terms: the self is both continuous with and separate from that which is not itself, which,
except for moments of communion, appears to it as impersonal.
In addition to its ragged margins, which give it variety, the self
is internally diversified by its two directions of falling back upon
itself and overseeing its life, and of being drawn into the world:
Ortega's *ensimismamiento* (the "preoccupied" self), and *alteración* (the "occupied" self). Preoccupation draws the self
back into a compact center of awareness, a pure ego to which
all else is other, whereas occupation draws the self out into a
context of orientation in which consciousness becomes nearly a
constituent or a function of a wider activity.

Self is also an equivocal term with regard to its relation to
consciousness. In a primary sense it is not possible to speak of a
self that has not appeared in specific momentary experiences
as the center of a life it possesses. Indeed, at one extreme it can
be argued that the self is merely a momentary experience considered from the standpoint of the ego to which it belongs. In
such case there would be as many selves as there were momentary
experiences. In a sense this interpretation is true, because there
can be no self that cannot be actualized in a moment, and each
moment is a unique reality unto itself. However, the notion of
self goes beyond conscious presence and embraces tracts of life
dotted with self-conscious momentary experiences. At the extreme in this respect the self is an entity that persists even when
it is not actualized in an intuition of essence or in a lived present.
In the *Upanishads* frequent reference is made to the three modes
of the self: waking life, dreaming, and dreamless sleep. When
one wakes up in the morning one resumes one's waking life as
the same life it had surrendered by falling asleep the evening
before. Often waking comes abruptly on the heels of a dream,
which prolongs itself, and there is a sharp dissonance between

two modes of the self. But within that experience of dissonance there is still a single self, here a self-at-a-loss caught between two heterogeneous contexts of orientation, struggling to get out of one and into the other while both exert great attraction. What happens momentarily and instantaneously in abrupt waking is smoothed out when one wakes up slowly and lingers in a zone of reverie between waking and dreaming. In such a state the self keeps shifting back and forth between dream and waking imagination, and sometimes even accomplishes the feat of directing a dream to satisfy a desire of the waking self, which points to a mixture of the spontaneity of a dream and the deliberate design, indeed, usually ritual, of a fantasy. The zone of reverie reveals clearly the continuity of the self between dreaming and waking, though of course it is filled with momentary experiences of a distinctive character.

When waking does not proceed from dream or reverie it is felt as a recovery of a self that has been lost over a stretch of time, not as the birth of a new self. The first thing the emergent self must do upon waking is orient itself to its environing context: it comes into a context that it must make its "own" by drawing upon its past resources. Yet it is also wholly new, an entirely fresh actuality. The waking self, the dreaming self, and the self lost in dreamless sleep are the same yet radically diverse. They are the same in the sense of "mineness" that marks many dreaming and waking experiences, as well as through the judgment of a waking self that reflectively reviews the kinds of experience in which the self participates. Such a reflective review reveals dreamless sleep not as an "experience" but as a nonconscious mode of being that stands between certain conscious moments, and is indescribable in such conscious moments but necessary for them to assume. Although "my life" is grasped to be the radical reality only in a moment of acute self-possession, that does not mean that "my life" is confined to such moments. What is revealed to the centered self is the vision of a life proceeding from birth to death in which consciousness in different degrees of vividness and complexity dawns and then retreats into dusk. But from that same position of centricity the self can be collapsed into the confines of its privileged actuality, in which case that lived present seems to become all that the self is.

In the useful phrase of Martin Heidegger, the self is "proximally and for the most part" in between the extremes defined by the two sets of poles that form its boundaries. Most of an ordinary life is composed of waking experiences that evince neither the reduction of consciousness to a function within activity nor the transcendence of consciousness over the field it comprehends, and neither the entertainment of the span of an entire life nor the confinement to a vivid actuality. Ordinary consciousness, the self that is most familiar, skips over the actuality of any particular momentary experience without ever reaching the position of overseeing its life and, therefore, grasping it as a distinct and finite entity. The personal existent, attached to or merged with a body open to that which is external to it and vulnerable to danger, is a deeply practical being, ever searching beyond itself for that which might complete it and, most profoundly, make it invulnerable to harm. Personal existence actively transcends into the world when it is practical, utilizing what surrounds it to bring some object into a satisfactory relation to itself by making itself receptive, drawing other things or persons into itself, or transforming objects to suit its ideas. From this viewpoint, thinking is as practical as any task that involves muscular activity, because it is usually devoted to resolving some problem, to finding or generating some image or concept that will clarify the vague, define the indiscriminate, and fulfill the incomplete. The normal self is an operator, spilling over into the world to make it as much a home as possible, but holding itself back to monitor its interventions and effects. Ordinary consciousness is, therefore, an unstable synthesis of occupation and preoccupation, which arises spontaneously but is subject to dispersion as the specific objective that provides it with integrity loses its attraction or is actualized.

Ordinary practical activity, which alternates between the stand-points of actor and monitor, is continually breaking down into more sharply defined modes of activity that precisely display the structural components of the self. Although for the broad view of the self there is but one "I" that persists through momentary experiences, that center of experience is diversified into two egos, what William James called "the present acting self" and "the reflective self." Both are present in any conscious momentary experience and cannot be disentangled from each other, yet they can be analytically separated and then they appear to be partially superimposed upon one another. Instead of James's terminology, I shall use the terms "over-ego" and "substantial ego" to distinguish the two selves. The substantial ego, James's present acting self, is delivered into the world through the body; it is outside of itself and among other selves or objects, even when these objects and selves are the products of its own imagination. The substantiality of this self resides in its nearness to actuality, to the particular qualities characterizing each present. It is the point of contact of mentality with that which is external to itself, including other centers of awareness. The substantial self, being bound into specific situations, has a diversity within itself of personae, each one uniquely relevant to a given situation. It is a self suffused by feeling and emotion, responding primally to what it receives by a welcome or a rejection. In contrast, the over-ego is set back from direct involvement in the world through the body; it is with itself, gathered together, centered, and able to comprehend that which is not itself. The over-ego is an overseer, standing above life and assaying its contents, accepting them and not being reviled or revolted by them. It is not characterized by multiplicity but by a unity of conscious presence constituted by the act of gathering oneself into one's focal point of awareness.

The relations between substantial ego and over-ego are mutually inclusive: each includes the other depending on the viewpoint taken. From the substantial ego's standpoint, the over-ego is a monitoring function within an activity, a kind of servomechanism that regulates a performance. Here the over-ego is included in the substantial self as one of its components, more or less valued according to circumstance. For example, when the substantial ego is sleepy, the over-ego, which is self-conscious, is an annoyance at least and sometimes a sheer frustration. The substantial self regards the over-ego as an incident in its adventures, though one that is consubstantial with it and, after discipline, authoritative over it. From the viewpoint of the over-ego the substantial self is an aspect of a wider field that includes its environment and is not even, at moments when the over-ego is most precisely discriminated, at the center of that environment. The over-ego is the first "I" in Ortega's formula, "I am I and my circumstances" (*Yo soy yo y mis circunstancias*), the preoccupied self; whereas the second "I" is the occupied self, the substantial ego. The over-ego appears only when discriminated from the substantial ego. However, once the distinguishing activity reaches a certain degree of precision a qualitative turn occurs and a center of consciousness bathes and englobes a field in its light. The over-ego, which becomes distinct through ingathering, possesses a power of its own, a tolerance of experience that allows it to comprehend what appears to it and to check the release of overt activity or even the emergence of certain products of imagining and thinking. At its purest, the over-ego accepts all it surveys with equanimity, including whatever rebellion against it is fomented by the substantial self. It is guided by a compassion toward suffering and by a ruthlessness toward adversity.

The substantial ego and the over-ego do not necessarily conflict with one another. Insofar as the over-ego becomes clearly distinguished from its vital context, it can be satisfied with the substantial self when that self is not revolted by its life and, therefore, does not give way to destructive impulses, either against other objects and selves, or against the self. For the over-ego, the substantial self should be the protector of life, its own and others primarily, and an entity that enjoys life whenever possible: its principle is love of life and its constructive aspects, particularly all forms of delight and the ways of eliciting delight. Yet even though its principle is to restrain and, indeed, expunge destructive tendencies in the substantial self, its tolerance reaches beyond the bias of its own attitude to accept even that within the substantial ego which denies life and would lay waste to its own being. This higher acceptance of all of the phenomena that appear in personal existence, including those that are unacceptable, gives the over-ego an almost inhuman serenity, an intense indifference that allows, when it is most stringently cultivated, the substantial ego to show forth as the trickster it is. The over-ego does not displace the substantial self, but embraces it, surrounds it, while also maintaining a distance from it. When firmly discriminated, the over-ego gives the substantial ego maximum free play to respond concretely and fully to the particular situation and to mutate along with changes in the context of orientation. It is such letting-be that is ordinarily termed "trusting oneself," but it depends upon a process of making the substantial self trustworthy, which in turn is only set in motion by the risk of letting-be. In contrast to the over-ego, the substantial self has no substantive principle, but only the formal principle of satisfying the claims of whatever interest dominates it in each particular momentary experience. The substantial self cannot control the over-ego but can only swamp it by being carried away by the mood of a momentary experience and thereby reducing the component of conscious distance in it. The virtue of self-control is practiced when the over-ego is prominent in experience; it is the governance of the substantial self to orient it toward the protection and enhancement of life in the light of the inevitable destruction of individual life.

It is noteworthy that the over-ego, which tends toward pure awareness of a qualitative field, has its own substantive principle, whereas the substantial ego has none. In order for the over-ego to gain prominence, to be discriminated, the self must be in a mood of calm and peace which pervades the bodily feelings. This sense of serenity is not an influx into the over-ego from the substantial self—as Santayana, who was burdened by metaphysical naturalism thought—but the over-ego's own intrinsic mood. The idea that the over-ego is superimposed on the substantial self is confirmed by experiences in which within an atmosphere of calm the substantial self suffers and enjoys the most violent emotions or the most acute pains. It is the peace provided by the over-ego that makes it possible for the substantial self's tendencies toward what Matthew Arnold called "sweetness and light" to dispel anger, hatred, and resentment, first by allowing the destructive emotions to be expressed intensely, though without discharge into overt action, and then, when the emotional storm has ended, by focusing awareness on the promptings of good heartedness. The over-ego is a partisan of itself and of the substantial ego, whereas the latter is a partisan of whatever it happens to be at the moment.

In its fullest expression the self is the life of the embodied personal existent through its vicissitudes; in its essence the self is a center of conscious awareness of what is other than itself— the contents of that life—structured normally by the mutually inclusive relation of over-ego and substantial ego. The two egos must be analyzed as though they were disparate and, indeed, they appear to be so on close examination. Yet their disparity runs up against an even stronger assent to the unity of the ego, based on the vivid sense of the continuity of the self, which explains them as diversifications of a single entity. The relation between overall self and the two egos, and that of the two egos to each other comprehend the general characteristics

of the statics of the self. To fill out the elementary description
of the self, it is necessary to sketch its dynamics, the processes
by which it forms itself. The procedure followed here is that of
presenting an ideal reconstruction of self-formation from the
standpoint of the self that holds its life to be the radical reality,
observes the constitution of its conscious experiences, and com-
pares the elements that constitute different experiences. No
attempt is made to claim that the ideal reconstruction indicates a
temporal order of self-formation, such as a developmental psychology might give. Rather, it is based on a review of experience
from the inside. Just as the description of the statics of the self
was informed by a hierarchical image—substantial ego being
"below" the over-ego, and life being below awareness—so the
dynamics are also described in terms of a rank order, in which
this time the higher elements abstract from the lower ones and
yet add to and enhance them. Inherent to the order is a valuation
which makes the higher superior to the lower, in the sense of
its honor or, even better, distinction, which can mean both
discrimination and eminence, and here is used in both senses.
That valuation is free, not in the sense of being an arbitrary
determination within an open field of possibility, but in the sense
of being enlightened by the affirmation of life in view of sharp
awareness of its nurturant and destructive aspects.

Ideal but no guarantee or requirement

The foundation of self-formation is feeling, both in its
simplest variety—which is sensation—and in its more complex,
profound, and enveloping type—which is mood. Feeling is experienced by the ego as being both its own and, at least initially,
out of its control—indeed, spontaneous. The spontaneity over-
shadows the possessive feature of the experience to the extent
that one always finds oneself already in a mood, even if after-
wards one attempts to alter it. Sensation and mood adhere
closely to the body and are anchored to specific parts of it. Close
examination of a mood will reveal it to be an unstable synthesis
of a multiplicity of bodily sensations and fleeting images,

which when detached from one another compel the mood to be dispelled and cause another mood, usually that of calm detachment, however temporary, to take its place. Mood is intrinsically variable and mutable, as are the sensations that compose it and the images, often inchoate, that form the germs of its expression. A sufficiently discriminated over-ego will be receptive to subtle changes in mood and permit them to occur, thereby revealing an exuberant multiplicity at the foundation of the self. Those who in reaction to some trauma have clamped a rigid style upon themselves will screen out such multiplicity and permit only a few moods to be consciously illuminated. Mood is a preverbal and prereflective synthesis of conscious experience that indicates the autonomy of life from thought about it and, as Heidegger insisted, "attunes" one to one's existence, which is a "being-in-the-world." Such attunement is always valuative, reflecting desire, satisfaction, fear, or frustration. The object of self-control is not to suppress some moods and bring forth others, but to inhibit the overt expression of moods actuated by hatred and to soften those moods by the calm of the over-ego.

There is a conscious life from which words are absent, but it is not reflective or aware of itself as a conscious center of a life. Self-consciousness arises with the assertion of the substantial ego which comments on its moods and sensations; that is, it expresses them by representing them in sound. The first word, in this sense, is a vocal response to a complex of felt quality. That response is both part of the mood and an abstraction from it, a primary expression that sums it up. Through language, which depends upon higher processes than expressive response, symbols are further abstracted from mood and feeling and become conventionalized, referring without any inherent link to phases of the experiences below them. But comment is more basic than language; situations are expressed, encapsulated, judged, represented, and primally known through such responses as crying, laughter, moans, shouts, and coos. Language itself can be bent to the more primal expressive responses of the emergent self and, when perfected, can issue in poetry and prophecy. But that means that a personalization and concretization of a relatively abstract medium has been effected. Moods seem to impel an expressive response to fit them, an appropriate commentary on their significance for the self. Once such responses become frequent, the first traces of the over-ego—which is distant from immediate quality—appear. Primary expression of experience is closely identified with mood, but is more than mood, just as mood adheres to the body but is heterogeneous to it.

Above the process of expression is that of reflection, which abstracts from immediate response relatively stable meanings to which standardized words refer. Reflection gives the idea of a past and a future as real as the present and of a cosmos beyond the ken of any momentary experience and, indeed, beyond the self's own life. Reflection, which arises in the lived present to make references beyond it, may take the form of practical planning, historical reconstruction, or theoretical cognition. It permits one to design one's desired future and unifies the relatively disparate expressions of the even more diverse moods. In reflection the over-ego comes into greater prominence, but is subordinate to some idea of what the substantial ego should do or be. Expression draws the self toward the absoluteness of each present, whereas reflection comprehends many moments, either through condensing aspects of them into a concept or through comparing and contrasting them in the activity of temporalizing a life. Whereas the perfection of expression is poetry, that of reflection is philosophy, which reflects freely and comprehensively.

Both expression and reflection are verbal and compose the normal core of self-formation. The self, however, is not merely constituted by language and the ego is not a linguistic fiction, the word "I." Beneath expression is mood, which is preverbal; above reflection is contemplation, which is postverbal. In the process of contemplation, awareness is discriminated from all dynamized quality, not only feelings, moods, and images, but also the expressive comments on them and the reflective abstraction and arrangement of those comments in logical and temporal orders. Contemplation pushes beyond the over-ego. The "I" itself, as a qualitative respondent to quality, a speaker and a cogitator, becomes an aspect of the field of a more comprehensive and englobing self which is merely peacefully aware and neither comments nor arranges comments. Contemplative awareness is fully unitary, in contrast to the diversity of mood, expression, and reflection it englobes. Yet its unity is entirely transparent and, indeed, is null without its field. Self-control is at its peak in contemplative experiences in which there is tolerance of and distance from the other formative processes of the self. Contemplation is the fulfillment of in-oneselfness, because it accepts what the self is in its specificity without identifying with that particularity, as even reflective processes must.

If the fulfillment of in-oneselfness is contemplation, in which the personal center of consciousness is full enough that it seems able to impersonalize itself, its beginnings are in the act of the incipient self identifying with, taking into itself, a more discriminated and discriminating self. Though the method pursued is still one of ideal reconstruction, it is necessary here to use the language of temporal development. I know I achieved the discrimination of contemplation from the other processes of self-formation at a certain time in my life, and I must presume that I made my first identifications at an earlier time, though I cannot remember the experience. From the standpoint defined by the judgment that "my life is the radical reality," my first identifications are "rooted" realities in that life that I cannot remember, but believe in with real assent based on the evidence of my present repertoire of mental processes. "Real assent to primary identifications as formative of the self" means that we are primarily beings who express one another to ourselves;

though this activity stands higher in value, we are only second-arily beings who express ourselves to one another. Expression, indeed, is prior to identification, but the baby's cries and coos are not directed consciously at another self; they are simply responses to sensation and, perhaps, mood. The infant, how-ever, has an incipient self (another "real assent") that is elicited by the knowing care of elders. How it is possible for a self-conscious center of expression to emerge from a certain kind of nurturance cannot be understood in terms of any momentary experience that already contains such a conscious center; it can only be a matter for speculation. And, if only to reinforce the mood of the discussion, one might speculate that, as Freud thought, identification is the way to make up for the loss of an object of love. The infant must somehow be able to keep the other self as self, thereby gaining substance for and definition of its own self, though not yet distance from it. The expressive self is first a representative self, one that re-presents to itself the others who have made an impression on it.

The idea that we are beings who express one another to our-selves means that the free individual emerges or is brought forth (both alternatives compel assent) not only through the processes of animal life but also through those of sociality. How discriminated selves could have come into being in the first place cannot be answered in terms of a view that knows the self only as an emergent from identifications with other selves. One might speculate that the personal existent can emerge in situations in which the element of conscious concern in the care that is given is absent or barely present. But we do not even have mediate experience of those possibilities. The kind of reflective review of personal existence undertaken here follows Freud in designating identification as the primary act in the formation of the self-conscious ego. That ego is at first somewhat inchoate, a variety of responses that are not closely integrated with one another and not themselves precisely defined or discriminated. The substance of the self is enhanced day by day as the incipient ego appropriates the selves who care for it. Traumatic events, severe pains, and/or ecstatic pleasures associated with the protectors and nurturers are particularly significant in self-formation because of the problems they present for the impulse to identify. However, the major impact of those figures into whose direct control the new and undiscriminated self has fallen is in presenting a daily example of what it means to be a personal existent. The incipient ego is a *tabula rasa,* not with regard to feeling and even to the potentiality of making a knowing response, but with respect to the identifications it will be impelled to make through the impress of others upon it. Unamuno remarked that the human being is a "unique species" of selves. That metaphor is appropriate not only to the changes of the self from moment to moment in tempo with shifting moods, but also to the collection of identities of which the self disposes by virtue of its identifications. The very basis of the unique species is the set of primary identifications that allowed the ego to emerge as a center of self-conscious expression. The self first defined itself through these identifications and only later could detach itself from them and reach the point of reworking them to make them more distinctive expressions of a single "personality" (the appropriate term for Unamuno's "species" as a qualitative whole). There comes a time in some cycles of dream analysis when the dream's cast of characters more and more resemble oneself, whereas when the cycle began, the otherness of the others was obtrusive. Yet making the characters more homely does not deprive them of the personalities they have evinced throughout the cycle. Similarly primary identifications with whomever the self appropriated may be fashioned in later life to conform more to a design for living that has become self-conscious; but they will retain their substance in the self, as much when they are given play in imagination and overt activity as when they are negated by the mechanism of reaction formation: they are as much part of the personal existent as any bodily organ.

The multiplicity of identifications is the basis in the structure of the self for Freud's method of psychoanalysis, which means that each personal existent is also a diversity of persons. From the standpoint of a discriminated over-ego inspecting the vicissitudes of the substantial self, personality means an act—personification—which projects a particular style into a situation. At the acme of self-control the over-ego disposes of a repertoire of substantial selves, each of which can be unleashed in appropriate circumstances. New ones can be added to the collection in moments of imaginative creativity, and old ones can be muted when the overall mood of the personality shifts so as to make them relatively incompatible with it. At this high point of mental life the over-ego is free to be a trickster god because it deploys the multiplicity of the substantial self calmly and without hatred. If, however, the over-ego does not have such inner strength, the self will be drawn into some of its moods and the over-ego will collapse into the substantial self; this occurs most fully in states of delusion when actuality is expressed through the requirement of a single mood, the one William James called panic fear. Short of delusion is obsession, in which there is conscious distance from the stricken ego but little or no control over performance. And short of obsession are all of the fleeting projections in everyday life, through which each of us makes others actors in an inner drama of which they have no knowledge and of which we may even be unaware. Psychoanalytic method recovers all of the voices that make up the self and shows all those voices to be modulated in one's own key: it facilitates the withdrawal of projections and the acceptance of oneself as a whole and, thus, is a fundamental discipline of self-control.

Freud opposed to identification another direction of activity—cathexis—which corresponds in his lexicon to Ortega's *alteración*. Whereas in identification the self attempts to make itself similar to another personal existent, in cathexis the self moves outwards to fuse itself with another who is different from self, who supplements it by completing it with what it cannot provide for itself. The simplest instance of cathexis, perhaps, is the infant seeking out and then suckling at a woman's breast. Indeed, the baby at the breast may be thought to be merely symbolic of the life in the womb, which might be imagined to be a perfected cathexis. The movement outwards to gain supplementation and the pleasure that attends it is based in desire, which provides the more substantial aspect of the self with its dynamism. Desire in a broad sense includes its qualitative opposite, fear, which is a desire not to cathect. To avoid confusion, the term "interest" will be used to cover both fear and desire in a narrow sense—the movement to cathect. The multiplicity of the self is founded not only on the variety of identifications made by the personal existent, but also on the multitude of interests that determine the viewpoint of the self within its successive contexts of orientation. Interests are primally connected to the body and its requirements for sustenance. Later, symbolic completions—for example, praise—may become desired. They are not necessarily "sublimations" of desires and fears that are more firmly rooted in the organism, but have experienced qualities specific to them. The importance of the body as an initial locus for desire, however, cannot be minimized. The various life functions, such as respiration, alimentation, and elimination, are performed by different organs, each of which has particular feelings associated with it. Pain and discomfort call attention to the multiplicity of the organism, which is a pervasive context for the variety of the psyche.

Desire reaches down into those elements or levels of life that are not conscious, though in an unaccountable way. For biology, understood as a natural science, there are no interests but only processes, the successive phases of which are described most adequately in the terms of chemistry and physics. Desire and fear beg to be interpreted as phenomena of conscious life, be-

cause they are constituted by "lack" or what Jean-Paul Sartre
called "negativity." A desire for something or for someone
signifies that something that is wanted is not present, yet that a
positive indication of its absence is obtrusive. For the conscious
self, interest is expressed by a symbolic substitute for its concrete completion (for example, a hungry person thinks about a
meal) and by a feeling of strain (the hunger). It is difficult
to believe that desire does not characterize nonconscious aspects
of life, because we find ourselves, for instance, "getting hungry"
or "short of breath." Yet we cannot imagine how interests are
possible without an awareness of incompleteness, though not
necessarily a self-conscious knowledge of it. Fear is best considered in terms of its difference from desire. It may be conceived
of as inverted desire, focused on maintaining the integrity of
the self against external and internal threat. Desire goes out to
fuse with its object, whereas fear bends back upon itself. Yet
fear is not in-oneselfness, because it remains directed outwards
to ward off or eliminate its object, even when that object is an
alienated fragment of itself. Personal existents with whom the
self has become intimate almost invariably become objects of
both desire and fear at the same time that they become foci of
identifications. Indeed, identification may be understood as
grounded in a deep and originally inchoate desire to supplement
vital content with the more symbolic content of self-expression.
It has been considered here separately from desire because of its
unique role in constituting the expressive and reflective processes
of the self. The others with whom the incipient self identifies
are sources of new desires and fears for the self. The
self's desires and fears, in turn, help sustain its identifications.
The several kinds of multiplicity that compose the more substantial aspects of the self make any simple schemata of "self-
development" misleading.

For most of its waking and dreaming life the self is restless,
either driven by desire or assailed by fear, often fear of its own

desires and their expression. One conclusion reached by a reflective review of experience is that desire and fear exceed the self's ability to satisfy or palliate them. Indeed, the deeply rooted desire for invulnerability, which is a source of the most intense and abiding fears, cannot be fulfilled in any momentary experience. It can only be managed, more or less successfully, by diverting attention from it to other concerns—a symbolic substitute such as salvation or historical significance, resignation to defeat, or the effort to be acutely aware of the frustration of the desire to be able to affirm life limitlessly, yet to hold on to that desire. Most modern naturalists have analyzed the ways in which the self makes up for its vulnerability by seeking symbolic substitutions for its fragility. Santayana criticized the "pathetic fallacy," which he defined as the propensity of the ego to project the fulfillment of its desires into the cosmos. Dewey discussed the "quest for certainty," by which he meant the ideal fabrication of an immutable reality that is thought to stand behind the flux of momentary experiences, which is filled with changes, many of them abrupt and some of them adverse to the self. Freud was a master at identifying "defense mechanisms," through which the self resymbolizes its interests by attributing them to others (projection), altering their objects (displacement), modifying their content (sublimation), shifting their ground (rationalization), and negating their import (reaction formation). As a means of achieving self-control, psychoanalysis promotes the dismantling of defense mechanisms and the confrontation of the self with its own desires and fears. In particular, psychoanalytic technique furthers the withdrawal of projections from the figures to which they have become attached, whether they be other real personal existents or imagined characters such as those populating fantasies, dreams, and delusions.

Frustration of desires that, in principle, could be satisfied in momentary experience, subjection to abuse, and dawning recognition of the constitutive vulnerability of human existence all cause the corrosion of the mind that Nietzsche called "resentment" and that will be termed here the hatred of existence. Were it not for hatred, the problem of self-control would be simply how to train oneself to bear up to fears and excessive desires as long as they lasted, which surely is not simple but at least can be achieved from time to time. Hatred of existence creates a permanent disposition to be revolted by one's own life, objects in the world, and other selves. It is the result of having given way to the adverse aspects of existence so that the destructive potentials of nature obtrude into awareness continually, driving the substantial self to identify with these potentials through tendencies that, at their extremes, are homicidal or suicidal. Hatred of existence is the mood that suffuses the denial of life and may be associated either with Sartrian "nausea," which is revolted at a disorderly world (the world as it appears when the pathetic fallacy has been burst), or with Kierkegaardian "dread," which quails at the self's instability and fragility. A persistent propensity to hatred of existence ordinarily leads to what Nietzsche called *ressentiment,* the detraction from virtue in the name of the superiority of weakness and compromise, the attempt to justify giving way to destruction. Self-control is the fundamental virtue because it is directed at containing and eventually eliminating the hatred of existence. The other virtues, artistry and love, depend for their fulfillment on the tolerance and discipline that self-control provides.

To be able to tolerate and later to mute the hatred of existence, it is necessary to expose that hatred in all of its depth and intensity to self-conscious awareness. For the most part the self protects itself from acknowledging its revulsion against its life by means of what Freud called "compromise formations." The extremes of panic fear, which most people have felt at least several times, show why the mind needs such healing mechanisms as the various symptoms of classical neurosis and psychosis, forms of psychic scar tissue. It is common for people to wake up from a nightmare at the point at which they are consumed by panic that they will be overwhelmed by overpowering forces. At the very depth of that fear, indeed of all fear, which is on the road to panic, is the super-added fear that one will submit to those forces, deliver oneself to them, let them ravish and rape. That one will surrender, relax, and let destruction do its work, is the greatest fear of an organism that cannot help fearing its vulnerability. One may hate one's life sufficiently, because of the fear that pervades it, to wish no longer to stand out against the world: it is against the death wish that the defense mechanisms mobilize. The autist, one may speculate, has become terrorized enough by existence to take the desperate expedient of obliterating the sense that there are any realities independent of the self. Other forms of psychosis are more affirmative of realities independent of the self and, therefore, are compromise formations between the affirmation and the denial of life. For example, homicidal psychoses are projections of self-hatred onto others, whereas paranoidal delusions incorporate denial of life, through the sense of victimization, and affirmation of life—through the will to oppose and outwit projected enemies. Beyond psychosis, along the way to affirmation, are the classical neuroses, in which the self experiences various "secondary gains" (charges of pleasure) from a symptom that restricts the self by possessing it and ritualizing it (preventing it from responding freshly and with a welcome to new momentary experiences). Psychosis makes the whole mentality scar tissue, whereas neurosis is a localized scar the self keeps picking to feel the irritating pleasure, the thrill of a fear that is always flaring up but never sufficiently threatening to drive one to annihilation. And, finally, beyond the classical neuroses are all of the forms of what Santayana called "normal madness," the stories we tell to convince ourselves that the world is our home.

The most sublime conceptions of an eternal unity of being, such as appear in the *Upanishads* or in the writings of Plotinus or Meister Eckhardt, are nearly transparent scar tissue. Other philosophies that make the cosmos a unity are on the way back toward neurosis.

The hatred buried under all the protective layers the self has built up can only be exposed by criticizing the various "compromise formations," which, in Alfred Adler's terms, are also "compensations." One must discover what one's psychotic interludes, neurotic rituals, fantasies, and pet prejudices and peeves are making up for, covering over, representing, and checking. A compulsive ritual—for example, caring for a machine with overscrupulous attention—may turn out to be a reaction formation against the desire to destroy that machine, which is making one's life tedious, dangerous, or demanding. One will not know whether that is the case, however, until one has criticized that ritual, first by acknowledging it to be symbolic of something else and then by interpreting the symbol in terms of its referent. It is Freud's central contribution to the study of the self to have discovered—for it was a discovery not an invention or innovation—the most thorough method of self-criticism. The Freudian revolution in the understanding of the self was not theoretical or experimental, but strictly methodological. What Freud discovered was that people can understand their own symptoms if only they relax enough to let their imaginations freely associate with the content of the symptom. Here, I take it, is the hardcore Freud. What he added on to his discovery to justify it theoretically (the "unconscious," the "scientific myth" of the "primal horde," and the tripartite analysis of the mind into id, ego, and super-ego) and to turn it into a therapeutic program (the "oedipal myth," the "transference," and the stages of development of the sexual impulse), I do not find essential to the task of self-control. Indeed, these additions impede one's recognition of one's own special and peculiar exercises of imagination, deflecting particular acknowledgments into general categories. It is the individualizing and personalizing aspect of Freud's thought that makes it an aid to virtue.

Free association is a radical departure from normal therapy, which intervenes from the outside to effect a change. Treatment of neurosis through hypnosis and suggestion, an interventionist approach to which Freud's practice was an alternative, is a form of what Heidegger called "leaping-in" to save the other, whereas encouragement of free association is a form of "leaping-ahead" that creates a permissive environment for fuller self-expression. Continuing the comparison with Heidegger, the method of free association is a "letting-be" of the patient, a trust in the patient's self-diagnosis, so long as that diagnosis is achieved by the free imagination. If I am correct that the essense of psychoanalysis—what makes it a unique form of understanding—is the method, or even better, the technique of free association, then in its most perfected form psychoanalysis is self-analysis. The self that in its own solitude can let its imagination play upon the images that appear in its dreams, that can identify with the characters in those dreams and speak spontaneously in their voices while awake, need not have recourse to a therapist in order to conduct analysis. Indeed, psychoanalytic technique is apt to work its most impressive results on those who have strong egos, in the sense of being able to discriminate, at least for extended periods of time, the over-ego from the substantial self. The less one needs psychoanalysis as a therapy, the more one is likely to derive from the use of the technique.

The technique of free association, when applied apart from any assumptions about what its substantive results will be, leads to knowledge of individual psyches, not to theoretical insight, except by comparing cases to find out what they have in common. Using stories, such as the oedipal myth, to make sense of the general development of the self is an example of what Alfred North Whitehead called "the fallacy of misplaced concreteness." Such stories may be useful summaries of the histories of certain selves that have arisen in specific circumstances, but they should not be used to anticipate what free association will yield in any particular instance. C. G. Jung, who carried out dream analyses in cycles that lasted months and even years, became convinced that each person is an epic poet singing a song of the self. That he then made Freud's mistake and tried to define a set of universal archetypes (his alternative to Freud's "scientific myths") need not inhibit others from drawing the conclusion that each epic poem of the psyche will express a unique history and will be populated by objects and selves that represent specific past events and highly particularized identifications, desires, and fears. Unravelling the significance of the epic depends upon: being cognizant that it is in a continuous process of creation; capturing its moments firmly in memory, particularly dreams, fantasies, fleeting images, passing compulsive gestures and obsessions, and inexplicable or surprising behaviors; and then being sufficiently unburdened by anxiety to set the imagination free to express the story more directly before an acutely wakeful attention. Just the ability to associate freely signifies a tolerance of oneself. Those who have attempted dream analysis know that the first barrier to practice is the difficulty in remembering the dream at all; once that is surmounted the next obstacle is taking the dream seriously enough to analyze it. Even after years of practice the initial response to a remembered dream will often be that it is not worth taking time to consider, that it is too trivial. To overcome resistance to analysis, one must have the inner discipline, the self-control, to focus attention on the remembered dream, despite the tendencies to divert it, and yet also remain relaxed enough to allow the imagination to play freely until its products draw closer to a direct expression of the interests the dream represents. Such militant acceptance of the self is a victory for the over-ego, which—through the practice of opening the way for free association—becomes more acutely discriminated from the substantial self as the self becomes more tolerant of the full range of its own expressions, especially those of buried hatred.

For Freud, the royal road to the unconscious was the interpretation of dreams. Indeed, the method of free association is best adapted to the study of dreams because the dream is the most complete product of the spontaneous imagination, the fullest expression of interests that have been suppressed in waking life. The distance from a dream to the interests and ideals it represents is shorter than that between the ritualized symptoms of neurosis and psychosis, and their motivational bases. Dreaming life, as noted above, is a state of being radically diverse from waking life, one that appears to be self-contained, a world unto itself. Freud's idea that the dream is a psychosis should be reversed to read that delusion is a dreaming while awake. Elias Canetti entitled the last section of his novel *Auto-da-Fé,* "world in the head," implying thereby that all experience is delusional. A view based on the declaration-proposition that "my life is the radical reality" cannot agree with that judgment, because such realities as other selves, things, the past, and the future—which are rooted in my life—are too obtrusive to deny. What gives delusion its importance is that it shows that I can turn away from the rooted realities and fall back on imaginative and imaginary projections, that I can dream while awake. Dreaming life is encompassed by a "world in the head." In the dream I experience a concrete solipsism; the momentary experience or set of experiences that form the dream are populated usually both by myself and other selves; yet from the perspective of a waking life refined by dream analysis, all that appears in the dream is the product of the self. That the objects and other selves in a dream appear to the dreamer without the stamp of their authorship means that the self has not become integral, has not been able to tolerate and discipline itself sufficiently to express itself with one voice modulated in many different keys. Dreams, indeed, may be most comprehensively understood as the vehicles by which aspects of the self that are denied expression in waking life have their say, though most often in symbolic form. In other words, in the dream the self encounters itself as a wider whole than it does when it is wakeful. Dreams, therefore, are self-referential; they are not subordinate to waking life, mere comments on events of the day before or of years ago, though they are that too. Most important, dreams are those experiences in which the self confronts what it has become in itself rather than what it is in response to the realities that are rooted in its waking life. Broadly defined, the self includes wakefulness, dreaming, and dreamless sleep. In dreaming the self is closest to itself, which means that the interpretation of dreams is the royal road not only to the unconscious but also to self-control.

In the dream the multiplicity of the substantial ego takes the form of a dramatic performance, even if at one limit it is just one scene, a soliloquy, or an image. The dreams in which the self reveals itself most fully are those most like theatrical productions, many scenes populated by a cast of characters. The key to dream interpretation is to consider the dream as a work of art, the most general sense of which can be gained—by means of free association—by naming its pervading mood or moods and assigning it a title, which by virtue of its spontaneity it could not give itself. Dreams, indeed, are not entirely works of art because their meaning or import is not determined until their last frame has appeared. And often through a single night or through a succession of nights the same message will be conveyed in a sequence of dreams in the self's effort to express it precisely. Once the drama has been named and its feeling-tone fixed, the characters, their relations to one another and to the self, and the objects in the environing context can be understood according to their import for the whole. The cast can be divided into those figures with whom the ego identifies and those with whom the ego cathects, and cross-cutting that division into those who are on the side of the ego as presently constituted and those who want to dethrone it and seize it for themselves. As dramas, dreams are adventure stories in which ego struggles against rejected identifications and cathexes, often allying itself with former opponents and thereby altering itself and giving the waking ego a new temperament based on a new synthesis of interests. The general strength of the ego as possessor of its own life is indicated precisely by how well it fares in its dreams against the assaults of its opponents. Nightmares indicate a weak ego that most likely has to ritualize daytime activity in order to avoid overt expression of rejected interests. Dreams marked by a feeling of power show at least a momentary integration of the self's multiplicity. Special dreams that occur during cycles of dream interpretation show the structure of dreaming itself and present the formal aspects of the self to itself. Sometimes the imagistic character of the dream becomes dominant, as when the dreaming ego is discriminated as a self-conscious over-ego that arranges frames of imagined quality in a sequential order, often substituting one frame for another to secure a proper ending. Here dreams appear as constructs, works of art. In other cases the dream is so attractive to the ego that it is drawn into it as into an abomination and must fight to wake up. Here the dream appears in its aspect of separate and spontaneous reality. Finally there are dreams in which over-ego is fully discriminated from substantive ego and watches the substantive self perform an activity, passing judgment upon it. Such dreams replicate the distinction in the *Bhagavad-Gita* between Krsna, the rightly disposed advisor and overseer, and Arjuna, the warrior who must effect the actual occurrences that have been disposed.

As a cycle of dream interpretation proceeds systematically over several months the *dramatis personae* in the many dreams become more and more familiar, and finally are recognized as members of a single repertory troupe that performs night after night, not always in the same drama but always in one adapted to the characters and temperaments of its members, that is, to the complexes of interest, mood, and expressive voice they represent. Perhaps, in this sense, dreams can better be compared to television series than to single plays. Indeed, they become more so as a cycle of interpretation proceeds and the masks of the characters become less alien and resemble more oneself and those persons who were in charge of the self early in its life and supplied it with its primal identifications and cathexes. A cycle of interpretation begins with a vivid and impressive dream that often is complex and arrests the attention of the self as it awakes. The cycle moves through vicissitudes in which the ego rises and falls in strength, friends and foes are distinguished, and coalitions are made and unmade. The ending is frequently a simplification of the initial conflict, in which the multiplicity of original interests is reduced to a sharp opposition between two of them, an affirmed identity and a rejected identification. Indeed, the revenge of rejected identification is a primary motivator of dream life. As a cycle of interpretation proceeds, the stakes of the struggle are raised as the self criticizes all of the compromise formations that have satisfied in some part the claims of the rejected identification, and as that which the self was rejecting is given precise expression. At that point the rejected identification may appear as the "double" of the self, someone who resembles the self but stands for all it abhors, yet who is a powerful component of the substantial self and, thus, attracts the self as a whole. The double may attempt to take over the substantial ego and destroy the over-ego, which means that the double is not only defined formally as rejected identification but also substantively as the representative of the desire to give way to fear and, thus, of destructive tendencies and the hatred of existence. Dream interpretation leads directly to the test of one's ability to tolerate one's impulses toward destruction and, once they have been exposed starkly, to inhibit them from overtaking the self.

Psychoanalysis may be considered as a methodology for containing hatred, that is, the evil proceeding directly from the self as opposed to the destructive consequences that proceed from Dionysian excess. The root of evil is the vulnerability of the self to destruction, which is a constitutive element of the self and, thus, an objective condition, in the sense that no wishful thinking on the part of the ego can eliminate it. Here evil is understood in a broad sense and has nothing to do with the quality of an individual will. Hatred, the evil especially particular to the self, arises as a response to the adverse aspects of personal existence. The most concretely vital expression of such hatred is nausea, a revulsion against being as such, self and world. The "double" of the self represents the evil that the waking ego has rejected or sublimated, and that the dreaming ego has normally sublimated. The "double" would take over the ego in a bid to institute a perpetual reign of terror over the self and, ultimately, to an- nihilate all of the other members of the substantial ego. It would then have annihilated itself because its only principle is abstract domination, which at its limit is the enactment of the ability to destroy. Hatred, the mood that accompanies the impulse to annihilate, appears as the ego gives way to the temptation to deny life, to strike out or be stricken. The evil of the self can be understood as cooperation with destruction, a definition that accommodates both the Manichaean and Au- gustinian sides of the issue. The Manichaean position is the more profound one because it acknowledges the objectivity of the destructive element in nature—though it does not penetrate to the insight that evil is ultimately self-destructive. That objectivity is evinced in the self by the spontaneity with which the mood of hatred wells up in momentary experience. The self cannot obliterate the evil impulses within itself—they are consubstan- tial with itself—but it can attempt to control their enactment and even their prolonged expression by reinforcing the dis- crimination of over-ego from substantial self. It is only when the over-ego gains some prominence that the Augustinian interpreta-

tion of evil gains force. When one gives way to the temptation
to annihilate, one is falling from a superior to an inferior state of
existence: one is drawn into one's own dismemberment. Here
evil stands out as a negative, as a deprivation of being, because
the fullness of experience—marked by an over-ego discriminated
from a substantial self—is diminished. The objectivity of evil
means that psychoanalysis cannot eliminate the hatred of
existence or even lessen its intensity, but it can help bring that
hatred into sharper focus and thereby contain and isolate it. The
danger is that containment and isolation make the hatred all
the more intense, forcing a confrontation between the self and
that which it has rejected, but which is still part of the self.

For the most part, in waking experience, the destructive tendencies in the self are not expressed directly but are altered in
their conscious appearance by the operation of various defense
mechanisms. The responses of panic fear and of revulsion
against existence are most often disguised by what may be called
the rebellious or defiant ego, the "me." One may speculate that
the sense of a "me" that stands over and against the world (and
such a posture of negation and rejection may be essential to the
discrimination of over-ego from substantial self) arises from
the experience of the child's feeling betrayed by its protectors and nurturers, and responding by self-assertion. Such
self-assertion is always exercised against the traitors, but it also
rises above them by regarding them as rooted realities within the
self's life. But children are so dependent on their keepers that they
cannot stand the isolation of standing over them and are
caught in a countertendency of attraction. The child may run
away from home and then come back; or may think of suicide as
a way to make its keepers regret the harm they have done. The
future destiny of the self is greatly influenced by the way in
which the defiant ego—the wounded child with infinite perspectives before it—becomes a feature of the substantive self. One
resolution of rebellion—given far more attention than it war-

rants, inasmuch as it is not a pervasive feature of personal existence—is the formation of a counter-"me" that suppresses defiance in the name of conformity to commands regulating conduct. In the present perspective what Freud called the super-ego is not, as he thought, an internalization of commands from the outside, not even an identification with a keeper, but a reaction formation against rebellion that transmutes panic fear into guilt. The rebellious ego that will "go it alone" or "show them a thing or two" need not be stifled by reaction formation, but may also be sublimated into some sort of seeker of power or wealth or prestige, or into a self-deprecating depressive, someone consumed by shame. Pride and shame are the two poles between which the current of evil alternates in the normal waking self. They are expressed and enacted along the axes of master-slave, homicide-suicide, mania-depression, and sadism-masochism. The defiant ego—which was best described in literature by Dostoevsky through his figures of the "underground man," Raskolnikov, the"raw youth," and Ivan Karamazov—leaps between the poles of destroying or diminishing the other, and destroying or diminishing the self. In sociology defiance makes its appearance in the "authoritarian personality" that reacts with servile obedience to superiors and tyrannizes its subordinates. Most adult selves are characterized by a weak side that vacillates between the two extremes of annihilation, without coming close to reaching either one. Their evil is controlled not by a super-ego but by their general affirmation of life, which allows them to recover rapidly enough from the wounds others inflicted on them to prevent their giving way to destructive impulses. The super-ego replaces the rhythm of cycles of weakness and strength in the self with a form of paranoia, specifically a concentration of evil into a guilty self that is punished by a conscience. A discriminated self does not resort to reaction formation, but to conscious restraint and cultivation of the affirmation of life. It does not deny its weak side, but once it has brought it fully into awareness seeks to bathe it in ironical humor, exposing its pretensions to grandeur or to abasement.

Although the "me" is the fragment of the self most significant to the understanding and achievement of self-control, it is only one of many faces and voices that characterize the substantial ego. The defiant ego, which separates the self from that which is other than itself by antagonism, has many guises but is not exhaustive. Also groping for expression by the self are all of what may be called, after Freud, the erotic tendencies that make for union of the self with the various realities rooted in its life. Such urges to union may be as illimitable as rebellion, but in the direction of Dionysian ecstasy, an excess of life that seeks to identify itself fully with its environment and yet retain in some way its discrete center of awareness (a demand impossible to satisfy because it is self-contradictory). A discriminated over-ego must not merely control evil but must also moderate its various erotic selves that are organized around complexes of desire and that thrive on a multitude of pleasures. The art of self-management consists in giving as full a play as possible to different erotic tendencies, making as much as possible of the totality of the self operative in each momentary experience, softening and blunting impulses to destruction, and ensuring that destructive tendencies do not infiltrate the erotic ones, subtly turning them to the use of sadism or masochism, mania or depression. Self-control, however, is not fundamentally an art but is a power of the self to discriminate itself into an overseer tolerant of diversity and of adversity, yet militantly benign.

For the exercise of its method, psychoanalysis depends on sufficient power to discriminate over-ego from substantial self. To associate freely it is necessary to separate oversight from the process of imaginative production, which latter shows forth as spontaneous and is not simplified—as is the case in practical

activity—by direction toward an explicit goal. It is not so much
that the method of free association is based upon an objectification of the substantial self, but that it reveals the complexity of
subjectivity by splitting it into a domain of content—around
which the substantial self gravitates—and an attentive activity
that comprehends the field of content, the over-ego's supervision.
Splitting subjectivity is felt as a power, a holding back of attention from involvement in any of the particulars toward which
it is directed, an effort-laden distancing—which effort is not
associated, as all others are, with muscular tension and release.
The indrawing effort requisite for the practice of psychoanalytic
technique, however, is not the most prominent feature of the
type of experience resulting from that technique. Psychoanalysis
is focused on eliciting suppressed interests, not on promoting the
ability to stand above life. Even as it cultivates watching and
listening, it is drawn toward the images and expressions of
which it facilitates awareness. The knowledge it achieves is of
what must be tolerated by the self if it is to control itself. But
that knowledge does not produce tolerance; indeed, as noted
above, the technique of free association can only be exercised
when one is tolerant of oneself. The "sense of power," which is
what Nietzsche claimed issued from self-control, is not achieved
by knowledge but by discipline, which must involve a radically
carnal element. The self must learn to live with the interests
it has previously suppressed, but not release evil intentions and
tendencies into overt action. To do so the body must be tamed,
along with the moods and emotions intertwined and interfused
with its restlessness.

The most elementary and direct form of discipline is merely
renouncing something one desires, but that is in some way associated with one's giving way to destructive tendencies. Going
"cold turkey" on tobacco, alcohol, or sweets, for example, brings
the self into immediate contact with a claimant desire that
begs, cajoles, and intimidates in its pursuit of fulfillment. Re-

peated successes in overmastering a desire that threatens to become a drive, or in not giving way to a temptation accustoms the self, as Nietzsche teaches, to trusting in its strength. That strength is evinced in the ability to retain the discrimination of knower from field, even when feeling and mood are adverse to the peace and benignity that sustain the over-ego. The experience of renunciation is at the opposite pole from that of being transformed by knowledge. One is aware of all of the impulses to give vent to the desire, and all of the rationalizations of those impulsions that are expressed by the "me." These take the form of the claim that self-denial is martyrdom for an ego that deserves to satisfy its whim; but one opposes the release of expansive emotion into overt action by a sheer refusal or determination, indeed, will, not to give way, and not by any empirical, conceptual, or intuitive knowledge. Renunciation is perfected only when there is no resentment attached to self-denial; the discipline must be affirmed for itself, for its contribution to and, even more, its actualization of self-control, which means its affirmation of life. One stands above a desire most conspicuously when one renounces its fulfillment. However, resentment draws the self away from itself and outwards into feelings of superiority over others, hatred of other's happiness, self-pity, or even self-hatred arising from wavering commitment, the special problem of what Nietzsche called half-and-halfers. Renunciation is also perfected only when it is not supported by extrinsic rewards and punishments, including counterrationalizations, which are rudimentary reaction formations, and promises and threats, which cater to and, therefore, inflate the "me."

In the domain of fear, risk is the analogue of renunciation. A fear is never overcome until one actually exposes oneself to the object feared, whether external, bodily, or a thought, image, or mood. This is not to say that one cannot prepare oneself to confront one's fears by imaginative rehearsal or by exposure, when possible, to small doses of the feared object. However, to control fear involves a risky test in which the self is exposed to fright and tries to avoid giving way to panic. Especially in the case of phobias, the object of fear can only be demystified when, after having detached it from its associations and what it represents, one accepts it as part of one's field, "salutes" it, in Santayana's terms, as a rooted reality in one's life. Fears grounded in actual danger, however, must also be tamed sufficiently to allow their objects if not to be saluted, then to be tolerated for what they are, even if one attempts to avoid exposure to them. A good dose of actually endangering the self is necessary to perfect the virtue of self-control, which is exercised fully only when based on a comprehensive tolerance of experience—not on a restricted tolerance that keeps up some discrimination between knower and field by limiting what the self receives to whatever its equivalent might be of Epicurus's garden. How much peril the self must risk to master fear depends on the specific composition of the substantial ego. Sometimes the Nietzschian injunction "advance or perish" cannot be honored because the stakes are too high; one must sacrifice oneself so as not to give way to fear or be drawn into depravity. The experience of sacrifice is equivocal, because one may be reborn the next day, and, thus, not have perished at all.

Sometimes the elementary disciplines of renunciation and risk are unable to control the self from releasing the expansive emotions associated with hatred or with the excessive feeling of individual power, of a Dionysian excess of life. Then, more rigorous disciplines of control must be applied to force the self to face itself as a composite of external environment, feeling and mood, imagination, expression, and even reflection. One such discipline is taught in Eastern civilizations as "sitting." The essence of sitting in a posture such as the full lotus position for extended periods of time is to overcome the restlessness of desire and the stressful anticipation of fear by putting the body into as stable—that is, as immovable—a disposition of its limbs as possible. Sitting is a school of patience in which the most varied impulses to movement rise to awareness, and the most extravagant images attract attention, but in which all are pushed into the field and are contemplated with cool benignity by the englobing and comprehending knower. Sitting requires at the outset tolerance of the physical pain involved in locking one's limbs tightly together and superceding that pain by placing it in the field of comprehension. Similarly it demands accepting the hatred of existence, but also surpassing that hatred by tapping the ability to entertain it with irony. The discipline of sitting provides the self with a temporary and very precious victory over the adverse aspects of existence, in which these aspects are vividly present but do not consume the self. The victory is that of the indrawing power of attention that maintains its distinction from both the substantial ego and the body at the very moment at which these become most obtrusive by the steady check on releasing them overtly. Sitting tames the body by tying it up in such a way that it can be undone instantly, yet is stable enough to pose an obstacle to untying it to satisfy even its own demands: it is a daily practice of remaining patient in the proximity of impatience and, thereby, introduces one to the mobility, mutability, and spontaneity of the body and the psyche. Through an effort of indrawing, of placing oneself within oneself— indeed, of self-assertion against overt expression and release—the over-ego is released and at moments becomes an eye of calm in the storm of the substantial ego and the living body to which it adheres and with which it interpenetrates. Those moments themselves are the free gifts of self-control.

Self-control is a complex perfection of life that may be described in terms of a dialectical development of its forms. The first moment of the dialectic (form of self-control) is inward tolerance of one's moods, feelings, expressions, and reflective thought; the second is the inner check on release of destructive interests into overt action or even covert expression; and the third is higher acceptance of oneself as having lived a concrete past regardless of one's failures to respond affirmatively in particular momentary experiences. In "The Will To Believe," William James used the term "inward tolerance" to refer to the prime virtue of the citizen of his ideal "intellectual republic." James was most interested in genuine tolerance of selves by one another—gained through appreciative understanding—rather than in the conventional tolerance based on ignorance of and unconcern with the other. James was deeply moved by a sense of the accidental quality of personal existence and felt that as a particular substantial self, what he called a "present acting self," he could just as well be anything else. When he collapsed into panic fear and suffered his existential agony, just before he burst forward as a leading philosopher of his time, it was in the presence of a vision of an epileptic patient he had seen at a hospital: he was struck by the thought that he could be that patient or, at least, become him. James was seized by fright at the fragility of personal existence, its sudden and momentary nature, at his vulnerability. It was this he had to learn to tolerate, especially as it was reflected in other persons. As he developed that tolerance over years he came to consider his own life as a fragment of a mosaic, what Arthur Kroker calls a "movable mosaic," in shifting relation to other fragments, his pluralistic universe mirrored in a society of selves. Inward tolerance may be extended to accepting the selves that constitute one's repertory troupe, including those who represent evil, either as hatred or submission; and beyond that to feelings, moods, images, desires, and fears. In particular the despair over being closeted in a finite life—to which every self that is strong enough to have made itself possessor of its life is subject—must be borne patiently and not allowed to degenerate into panic fear. Solipsism-toward-death, which is what the deepest despair may be called, reveals its own truth about personal existence: that it is precious and brittle. Inward tolerance is born fundamentally of the adverse aspects of existence in light of virtue: the virtue of self-control is a good-in-itself for the self, and a good for others only incidentally.

Inward tolerance is a receptivity to the contents of life that depends upon fixing one's attention on those aspects of the substantial self that the dominant complex of waking egos, usually including the "me," strives to reject. In itself inward tolerance has no principle for restricting the release of any interests into expression or overt action, but would, indeed, be able to comprehend destructive actions in the fullest sense of "surround." Whether or not one cooperates with evil is not a matter for inward tolerance, the principle of which is to accept the contents it receives as they are, not under the aspect of a wish about or a fear of what they might be. Regarding the distinction between good and evil as the basis for inward efforts to inhibit evil is a separable dimension of self-control, its second dialectical moment. Irving Babbitt, the other great turn-of-the-century American individualist, used the term "inner check" to describe the more assertive, rather than receptive, form of self-control by which the substantial self is held back from the release of "expansive emotion." As did James, Babbitt attempted to describe personal existence from a wide base of concrete experiences. He taught that we know the inner check directly as a contentless power of restraint, a *frein vital* that functions as a counter-poise to the *élan vital*. The inner check cannot be merged into expansive emotion by reducing it to just another interest demanding expression and release, in this case the interest in not releasing something. Rather, the inner check is the form in which over-ego becomes discriminated from substantial ego as a center of a personal existence that oversees that existence. Through the operation of the inner check, good is discriminated from evil, the former being that which supports the over-ego's calm beneficence and the latter being that which collapses

the over-ego into the substantial self, including here moments of
Dionysian exuberance, which are destructive by excess of rapture
and not by hatred. The inner check may be understood as the
form of self-control through which the over-ego maintains its
distinctive mood and attitude despite, primarily, all of the
tendencies toward hatred of existence. Inward tolerance gives
the over-ego the substantial self in its fullness, whereas the inner
check turns back upon the substantial self to inhibit—but only
by a pure inward restraint—the release of destructive interests,
including as it becomes stronger, their expression and finally
their appearance, not because the destructive interests have been
repressed but because the self has learned to love and affirm
more, allowing hatred to be dispelled as a morning mist is
by the sun.

Evil in its broad sense, the adverse aspects of existence, is pervasive in nature and spontaneously triggers in the self a response of hatred that is essentially a cooperation with destructive
processes and tendencies. The perfection of self-control would
be the elimination of all impulses to hate without loss of the
determination to resist evils proceeding from external objects or
from other selves. Artistry, the virtue to be discussed next,
depends, indeed, on a propensity to supplement the world as it
is received in order to improve it, make it more satisfactory—
that is, to resist evil. The susceptibility to evil, however, is so
prevalent that the inner check cannot be the final moment of
self-control. Even the self strenuously committed to a discipline
will continue to give way to the temptations to cooperate with
destructive tendencies and will have to come to terms with its
authorship of deeds that it acknowledges as unacceptable within
the terms of the over-ego in its aspect of *frein vital*. A self that
has cultivated inward tolerance of life will have many opportunities to attend to the diverse faces and voices of hatred,
particularly when it has made familiar the technique of free
association. The inner check's failure to operate may evoke in the

self attempts to fortify self-control with reaction formation or behavioral conditioning through reinforcement, whether the incentives are "material" or "moral." It may also breed self-deprecation, which is merely an early form of giving way. To maintain itself purely in the face of the self's evil, self-control must absorb that evil into the self as its own—indeed, welcoming it as part of experience while refusing to identify with it as a precedent for the present or for future occasions: it must welcome past evil as evil, not as something excusable or excused. This steady embrace of the self's past as a whole is the polar opposite of the Pauline conversion that turns one into a "new man" who has received the spirit of love. Inward tolerance and the inner check are completed in the virtue of self-control by the higher acceptance of oneself, the inward power not to be demoralized by one's own evil—indeed, to make ironic sport of it so that one is emboldened to participate fully in the train of emerging momentary experiences.

The virtue of self-control is constituted by a reference of the self to itself that is achieved by discriminating over-ego from substantial self. Self-control is a freeing of the knower from the field, in the sense that the over-ego is not identified with any state of the substantial self but has its own mood of benign dispassion. The distance from specific responses to the contents of life that is attained through the exercise of self-control is the foundation of all the other virtues, because virtue has an essential element of the deliberate in it—that is, some self-consciousness. To practice any virtue one must be patient enough to go through the steps necessary to transform some contents of experience into others, whether by altering quality, relation, or both. There must also be a propensity to risk that one's participation in a chain of momentary experiences will lead to a disaster. And, more important, the inner check and higher acceptance must be sufficiently operative to inhibit impulses to deviate from the task at hand and to persist despite failures to inhibit, respectively. The role of self-control as the foundation of the other virtues is nowhere more evident than in the practice of the arts, all of which are characterized by purposive construction and manipulation—that is, they are practical, informed by *techne*. In the context of the structure of temporal experience, art may be understood as an arrangement of the objective contents of experience according to a purpose (whether that purpose is clear before the onset of the process of arranging, or develops out of that process) over a chain of momentary experiences. Artistry—which is the embodied perfection of the skill involved in the practice of an art, the artistic virtue itself—can only emerge if the self is patient enough not only to learn something difficult but also to tolerate the temporal rhythms of the specific objects that must be arranged, whether they are thoughts, expressions, feelings and sensations, or things apprehended through sensation. Even the most abstract concepts of metaphysics or mathematics must be thought out in their relation to other concepts, named, and communicated, if only by the self to itself. All of this takes time and concentration, the latter of which is not properly part of artistry itself, but of the achievement of self-control.

That art may turn back and enhance self-control was shown in the preceding chapter in remarks on the art of sitting, that is, of disposing the body's limbs in such a way that patience is readily cultivated. Self-control enters into sitting in the tolerance of and check on temptations to move, whereas sitting creates a permissive context for the enhancement of self-control by arranging the limbs so that the body is in its most stable position, that is, the one in which in waking life it is the least restless. No practical discipline of fostering self-control should be confused with the moments of inward tolerance, the inner check, and higher acceptance in themselves: the self must possess enough control to undertake the discipline, which is inherently difficult. In the first instance, the discipline itself—its artistry—furnishes an enhancement of the inner strength. Indeed, every art may be practiced as sitting is, to make patience conspicuous and to accustom oneself to it.

The structure of art became a philosophical problematic in
the twentieth century through the work of such thinkers as John
Dewey, Samuel Alexander, and George Santayana. Dewey's
Art as Experience, Alexander's late essays on art, some of them
gathered in *Beauty and Other Forms of Value,* and Santayana's
Life of Reason and later studies of poetry, religion, and govern-
ment form a rich deposit of thought that is relevant to the
discussion of the perfection of finite and conscious life and how
most generally it is possible to achieve it. The understanding
of art that guides the present discussion is fundamentally
Alexander's, though Dewey and Santayana would affirm its
major claims. For Alexander, art is most generally an inter-
mingling or mixing of "mind and material" in such a way that
the material is transformed according to the mind's design—but
the mind must adapt to the particularities of the material. The
different arts are distinguished according both to how the mind
arranges the material (the principle of the order the mind gives
it) and what specifically the material is. In terms of Alexander's
view science, statecraft, social ethics, crafts, and professions are
arts or complexes of arts. What is generally called "fine art" is a
group of pursuits, such as painting, sculpture, and poetry, that
mix mind and material to create a significant and satisfying object
that appeals in a concrete and sensory way, but impregnates the
sense with meaning, makes it significant in itself. The broad
definition of art suggested by Alexander is weighted in favor of
fine art, because the fine arts show the most marked interpenetration of mind and material, and, therefore, are the
paradigms for the other arts, which look beyond their objects to
further results. Science, for example, fuses mind and material
in the movement from observation, through hypothesizing and
theorizing, to experimental testing. Yet even the "grounded"
theory is not self-standing, because it is open to further con-
firmation or disconfirmation, and may contain gaps between its
primitive theoretical concepts and the more qualitative definitions

of its experimental objects. Fine art is a stopping point within the flux of life that shows the finitude of momentary experience by forming an object that attracts attention for its own sake, not for its contribution to something else, including the desire and determination to preserve it. A painting, for example, should simply be worth seeing. Insofar as personal existence itself is made a fine art, it cultivates each of its momentary experiences as presents worth living in and for themselves whatever else they may procure.

The distinction between mind and material that makes art intelligible is subordinate to the discrimination of over-ego from substantial self. Once one practices the virtue of artistry one is necessarily delivered over to a practical activity and is, in Ortega's sense, primarily "occupied." Any preoccupation is really a phase of the occupation—that is, one may stand back from the physical acts involved in preparing a meal to scan one's ingredients and to consider whether to alter their proportions from what was specified in one's initial plan, or to add to or subtract from the list of ingredients. As John Dewey insisted, the thinking involved in such a pause is as integral to the practice of an art as are any of its behavioral operations. In the pursuit or practice of each art there is a unity of theory and practice, because theory is a kind of practice that departs from and leads to other phases of the conduct of the art in question. Art can interpenetrate mind and material just because the levels of the self-process are at least tangent to each other: expression represents moods, feelings, and percepts; and reflection orders expressions into relations of ulterior meaning. Art merely makes the interrelations of the components of the process of experience precise and, thus, conspicuous through the requirement that the self use its mind to help bring some of those interrelations to specificity and actuality. Both as a foundation and a perfection of artistry, the discrimination of over-ego from substantial self forms a context for the practice of the arts. The more the

observer is freed from servitude to the occupied self, whether the
latter be reckoning or performing, the more the art appears
to the self as a finite activity with a limited result that has its
own particular perfection and criterion of success. It is only in
such a state of experience that artistry stands out as a distinctive
virtue and the arts themselves become the objects of unalloyed
interest in their special perfections. The discrimination of
over-ego from substantial self takes away from art any preten-
sion to infinitude or transcendence, but gives a depth and a
seriousness to each instance of the practice of a specific art.

Civilization is the self-conscious practice of the arts, and its perfection is their self-conscious practice as arts—that is, as finite
pursuits with finite products, each of which may be judged by
specific criteria of success that define its perfection. This
definition of civilization makes modern Western civilizations
the standard by which others are identified and evaluated,
because it is only in the West that the various pursuits that
make up society have fully broken loose from reference to some
total transpersonal meaning. There could have been artistry, the
perfection of the practice of an art, in premodern civilizations,
but there was not the affirmation of the arts as worthy in themselves and of their perfection as an end-in-itself, one of the
major distinctive virtues. This is not to say that the West is
fully civilized, which is far from the case, but that only in the
modern West is society sufficiently differentiated institutionally
to permit the development of fully autonomous standards for
the different arts. That is, the notion that artistry itself is the inward and intrinsic motivator of the arts can readily occur to
people who are practicing arts, the standards of which relate to
the object being brought to actuality, and not to any reference
beyond it, such as ritual provides. One might label as Apollonian
a civilization that was based only on the affirmation of arts as
worthy for their own sake and not on any transpersonal

meaning, whether biological, historical, or supernatural. The
arts curb Dionysian ecstasy by guiding it into an *élan* for
bringing into actuality a certain accomplishment with a definite
form (though that form may be defined within the performance
itself). The arts crystallize the cloud of expansive emotion
into alertness.

As do the other virtues, artistry incorporates the affirmation
of life, but in the specific form of a love of one's own power to
plan and to execute, that is, to achieve a purpose that brings the
environment into line with a design. Even the arts of destruction
are life-affirmative, in the sense that they can be practiced as
arts, as ways of making material bend to mind. Nothing in the
concept of civilization suggested here excludes from it the arts
of war, which may function to extend the scope of an organized
society or to protect its territorial integrity. Indeed, one of the
definitive works of Hindu civilization, the *Bhagavad-Gita,*
is devoted to a conversation between Krsna and the warrior
Arjuna, who must be convinced to practice the military art,
though he is appalled at fighting a battle for which he sees no
justification and in which he will have to kill friends and
relatives. Among other things, Krsna tells Arjuna that he should
simply concentrate on being a good warrior and not be concerned with the consequences of his actions. The assumption
appears to be that Krsna takes care of the consequences, but
even that becomes unclear when he reveals to Arjuna the
"universal vision" that contains the works of both the nurturing
and destructive forces of nature. In light of the universal vision,
the *mysterium tremendum et fascinans,* the only reason for
Arjuna to go into battle is because his specific art is that of the
warrior, and to practice that art well will enhance his self-
control, his ability to discriminate over-ego from substantial self.
That discrimination will be effected by attending to the practice
of the art for its own sake, exercising the virtue of artistry,
which will put Arjuna into the mood of benign indifference.

The inclusion of the arts of destruction in civilization raises the question of whether there are any intrinsic limitations on the exercise of the virtue of artistry. Considered abstractly, artistry is not determined by any specific contents and is fully relative to the particular mixture of mind and material that has been purposed in a certain case. One might suggest that the idea of civilization itself includes some sort of principle of general welfare or of respect for individual rights, but that would imply that the self-conscious practice of an art would be civilized only if it were undertaken with a certain moral intention or for a moral aim. There is no general objection to defining civilization in terms of certain ethical principles, as such thinkers as Sigmund Freud and Alfred North Whitehead have done. That approach is not taken here because the wider view in which the present discussion of artistry is embedded derives morality from love, the virtue that perfects the relations among particular personal existents. The virtue of love is independent of artistry, though it only reaches its purest expression when the arts are practiced as finite pursuits. In a virtuous life artistry is limited by love—that is, only those arts that are consistent with love are practiced. Love itself is not an art, but a cherishing of the individuality of the other self for its own sake, a concern not to form the other self but to let that self find its own way most effectively to a virtuous life. Just as there are disciplines associated with self-control, there are arts of love which can and should be practiced with artistry. Those arts are properly parts of civilization, which is defined here in terms of a relation between mind and material, not between self and self. Interpretations of civilization that are informed by moral principles tend to combine the impersonality of art with the personality of love, confusing morality with adherence to general norms or laws, which are, indeed, products of the art of legislation, but which need not be based on a concern for the *hombre de carne y hueso,* the personal existent.

Artistry's formal indifference to its content is not limited by any internal moral principle, but does find some intrinsic restriction in the attitude that is necessary to sustain it, which is one of concern for the perfection of a task. The *Bhagavad-Gita* favors for the most part an active discipline of what might be called detached deliverance to the pursuits of life, which is the appropriate attitude with which to practice arts self-consciously as arts: in order to cultivate artistry, one must bind one's thoughts, expressions, and moods into a purposive activity, a performance, even if that performance is merely thinking about something clearly. Yet one must also be aware that the performance is a limited component of the field and, therefore, expect nothing from it but its own actualization either as a step in a wider finite act that may or may not reach fruition, or as a finite perfection sufficient in itself. Although from an abstract viewpoint it would seem possible, for example, to practice torture as an art—that is, with an artistry informed by detached deliverance—such an achievement would have to overcome the evil or the revulsion against evil that seem normally to adhere to such a pursuit as torture, to motivate it or to make its practice exceedingly difficult, respectively. Implication in torture, though not the performance of any physical acts, can be done with great artistry, as Adolf Eichmann demonstrated, and presumably there can be torturers who practice with artistry. Perhaps they can even have a benign outlook, gained by restricting their attention to their proficiency, to the affirmative aspect of their activity. It is the ability of destruction to gain a purchase on constructive impulses that constitutes the problem of civilization and that renders artistry incapable of exhausting virtue.

If knower could strictly and steadily be separated from field, there would be no hatred and, therefore, no evil. But because nature's ambivalence spontaneously sets off destructive ten-

dencies, the best one can do is repeatedly catch oneself giving way
or having given way, and then recuperate as quickly as possible. No art can entirely make up for nature's destructive aspect.
To expect one to do so is contradictory to the very virtue that
makes the practice of art possible: self-control. Self-control
checks evil first by tolerating the impulse to it, then by refusing
to release that impulse, and, finally, if one's resolve fails, by
accepting that failure with equanimity. Expectations that art can
fulfill personal existence also are oblivious to the virtue that
perfects it—love—which returns to the self, to intimate
subjectivity, through another self. At this point in the present
discussion art falls entirely under the influence of love, because
a judgment is made that in the total scheme of virtues the purpose of art is to serve love, not to serve itself entirely and
not to serve an abstract and unattainable goal of transpersonal
perfection at all. Civilization is not an end in itself, though
defenders of the legacy of ancient Athens tend to make it so. All
the ways of affirming life constitute the total end, in solidarity
with each other. Self-control makes the other two possible, and
artistry and love perfect life and, thus, render easier the
operation of self-control. Under the aspect of love, the arts are
defined in terms of their contribution to personal existence, that
is, to individual existents who can utilize and enjoy their objects:
each of the arts performs a function in human life that stands
out as special when viewed in terms of how it serves finite
individuals. The arts can be corrupted by evil and, thus, can be
diverted from their constitutive purposes. And there are arts that
do not belong to a good life, such as torture or propaganda.
One major aim of a philosophy of civilization is to present an
order of the arts in terms of the perfection of life. Here the order
will emphasize the components of the substantial self and the
over-ego in the respective arts, the basic arts being close
to the substantial self and the reflective arts being more distant.
    The most basic of the arts involve meeting the demands of

the body for sustenance and getting along with others expertly enough to gain that sustenance as well as the good that John Dewey regarded as the zenith of sharing in a common experience: acknowledging others and being acknowledged by them. What the fundamental arts are and how they are performed vary from one society and historical period to another: in small and nonliterate societies most of the arts are fundamental, whereas in certain sectors of contemporary Western societies and Japanese society, the fundamental arts seem in danger of disappearing altogether and being supplanted by highly automated technology. Fundamental arts in contemporary American society—such as speaking on the telephone, cooking, personal hygiene, driving a car, simple repair, and keeping an orderly account of and control over one's finances—illustrate the relativity of the concept of fundamental art. In each of the cases just cited one is made aware of the dependence of oneself on concrete external realities and on the body, but only in the context of technologies one could not construct for oneself. In the future new technologies may demand new fundamental arts, though the tendency of American social dynamics is to eliminate a body of general sustaining arts practiced by a large segment of the population and to replace them with service industries, which in turn are as automated or at least as streamlined as possible. If one is financially privileged one need not practice any of the fundamental arts listed above: Howard Hughes seems to have approached this state of life in his later years, and many who inhabit today's middle classes are on the way to it. Were the fundamental arts to be diminished further in contemporary American life, the virtue of artistry generally would become far more difficult to develop, unless supplanted by sport, crafts, games, and the reflective arts.

In the absence of the need for artistry in everyday tasks, the "me" is not tempered by the obduracy of rooted realities, the self-control attendant upon artistry does not operate, love seems

cheap, and there is little opportunity for the masterful unity
with things to develop, the sense of power that supervenes upon
detached deliverance. Artistry's special contribution to the
vitality of the personal existent is the strength that is felt and
produced in a controlled release of activity in which a task is
successfully completed. The virtue of artistry unites one to
things but puts them within one's ken. Fundamental arts are
particularly important because they delegate the requisites of
one's everyday existence partly to one's own initiative and, thus,
to one's liberty. The dread many people have of institutionaliza-
tion often stems from the fear of not being able to care for
themselves, of not being able to practice the fundamental arts.
The art of cooking, for example, enables one to prepare food
specifically for the tastes and nutritional requirements of oneself
and of those for whom one is concerned. Each fundamental art
also attunes one to particular qualities and their arrangements,
and, therefore, to beauty. Again, cooking gives sensory pleasure
in the preparation of each of the components and, of course, in
their combination in a satisfying whole. The relative independence from others gained in practicing the fundamental arts is an
important aid to becoming habituated to self-responsibility,
the grasp of one's own life as the radical reality. In a total
"service society" each would be patient to the agency of others,
and in some cases a specialized agent. One would participate not
directly, but only mediately, in one's own sustenance, and
would not become aware immediately of the totality of concrete
life to which the fundamental arts open one. Personal hygiene,
for example, grooming oneself well and caring for one's
minor ailments, reveals the body in its concrete particularity and
habituates one to attend to its signals closely, constituting a
tight interpenetration of "mind" and "material."

One of the great fundamental arts of American civilization is
driving, which I will discuss here as an example to illuminate
the structure of these arts. The art of driving essentially involves

safely conducting a heavy machine at high speeds under a wide range of road conditions. The artistry of driving involves perfecting the rudimentary skills of operating a car by taking automobiles into a wide range of situations: for example, into heavy traffic and onto ice and snow; getting out on the road in a wide variety of moods; and pushing the machine to its maximum safe limits, which can never be known until they are slightly exceeded, adding an element of danger to the process of learning how to drive a particular car virtuously. The artistry of driving demands the complete recognition that one's safety is entrusted to one's car, that one cannot stop at will, that a machine has become an extension of one's body, and that a car's parts can fail. Yet one must be close to one's car, feel it as nearly a part of one's body, make its movements responsive to one's discretion by getting to know those movements as well as those of one's own arms and legs. Practicing the artistry of driving makes the activity a good for its own sake, because one becomes sufficiently self-controlled and skilled to fear neither the road nor oneself on the road. The destination no longer makes a difference nor do the vicissitudes of the drive—poor weather offering a chance to exhibit and develop virtuosity, and traffic jams an occasion for an unexpected rest. At its peak of fulfillment the activity of driving gives one a unique feeling of being completely in transit yet totally in place, an at-homeness in the world gained from the ability to speed over a landscape in control of one's pace, to beat out traffic on a crowded expressway, to bounce over a country road, and to maneuver through a congested city. Driving is fundamental because it gives one access at one's own discretion to the facilities for sustaining everyday life in con-temporary American society. To be done well, so that it can serve that function of granting access fully, it demands not the cir-cumspection that propagandists urge but artistry based on testing the limits of one's ability to control the machine safely. Not only does the perfection of the art of driving give one greater skill and greater confidence, but it also releases one to the intrinsic enjoyment of the exercise of the art itself, the detached deliverance to the unity of psyche-body-machine, being fixed in motion. Were driving made too easy or too automatic, one of the greatest supports of individuality in American society would be lost.

The above discussion reveals one of the major reasons why the next art to be analyzed, that of politics, comes into being. The automobile is a dangerous machine which can be abused, that is, turned to the service of hatred or used with indifference to love. Within artistry itself, there is a Dionysian element of virtuosity that demands to see the limits of the art from the outside by breaking through them and thereby experiencing the failure of art. The urge to attain mastery may become so consuming in one who is inured to receiving the intrinsic joys of an art that endless efforts are made to press the boundaries of that art outwards. Philosophy honors such efforts on its own behalf, but not for any of the other arts, which is wise, because philosophy's empire is purely conceptual: the closest it gets to me is an abstract term such as "personal existent." The other arts also are not dedicated to being true to our lives, but have some particular services to render within life. It is assumed here that what is true to life is worth knowing and telling. This assumption is the gift to philosophy of an affirmation of life as it is, which, of course, can only be made fully when philosophy has offered its particular truths. The other arts affirm life through, in Dewey's terms, reconstructing it in one special way or another. Excess in their practice is trespass on the domains of other virtues, the totality of which in their appropriate exercise makes a good life. If human beings loved life fully enough to pursue its perfection single-mindedly, there would be no ground for political art. But they do not do so because they are prey to hatred and subject to excess. Within a civilization rooted

in self-control and purposed by love, the function of politics
is to protect the rest of the good life by placing an external
check upon the release of destructive impulses and certain
enthusiasms. But in a fully realized civilization there would be
no politics, which means that the positivism of political art is
exhausted in negativity in the same way that the healing arts are
directed against the destructive tendencies that impact upon or
are inherent to the body. Just as medicine cannot prevent death
and decay, politics cannot eliminate evil and excessive impulses,
but can only put up obstacles to their release. The moral root
of the acceptance of politics by the self is its acknowledgment
that it cannot trust itself or others to be virtuous, that obstacles
must be placed in the way of individuals to remind them of
what is essential to their good—that is, peace and proportion.

These observations on politics stress the police function as
paramount in political art. Politics places restrictions on the
release of impulse through control of space, by removing persons
or inhibiting external activities. Were means devised of localiz-
ing thoughts and products of the imagination, and of somehow
observing them or their specific corporeal dimensions, then
politics could attempt to control what is generally deemed
interior to the self. The chief means of control employed in
political art is the sword; physical coercion, direct action upon
the body, or, more frequently, the threat of such action. I find
Hobbes and Machiavelli unsurpassed in their understanding
of the art of statecraft, the former describing the structure of the
product of that art, the state, and the latter detailing its artistry.
Hobbes undersood how our vulnerability to one another sets off
a panic resulting in a "ceaseless search for power after power,"
and it only enriches his interpretation to base the salience of
that vulnerability on the insights of depth psychology into our
own hatred of existence which makes us constitutively distrust
ourselves. The state is a sword that hangs over us to protect us
from ourselves and each other. It is wielded by those of us who

seek to do so, which means those of us who are comfortable with its use. However far the state seems to wander from physical coercion, the threat of it is always near, and if it is not, then there is no state but merely some administrative facilities providing services for particular groups and individuals dedicated to specific activities.

The sword is used in politics to enforce decisions about what is to be permitted, required, and inhibited. Each decision is a determination of the character of the contexts of orientation of personal existents, the common and objective dimension of which may be called the "public situation," that field of civilized life in which selves meet each other, find a common ground. The basis of the state in our distrust of one another and of our-selves means that those who wield the sword, the governors, are no more trustworthy than we are, indeed, are probably less so because they are attracted by the coercive element in life. Lord Acton's dictum that absolute power corrupts absolutely is true because evil and excess are spontaneous and irreducible as are the claims derived from them of the "me," in its directly selfish expressions or in its more sublimated forms of group egoism. The state, the proper function of which is to protect the exercise of virtue, attracts all sorts of other projects, particularly those inspired by predatory impulses. It often becomes as great an evil or, perhaps, a greater one than those it was supposed to control. Statism, as Ortega noted, eliminates spontaneous adaptation in social life. Once one becomes accustomed to seeing the sword behind all of the other shows of politics, the thought of anarchy may become tempting. Why must there be a sword over us when it is wielded by people who are, in the main, less virtuous than we are? John Stuart Mill, working Hobbes's vein, answered that question by reminding us that there are also swords alongside us. That observation does not justify any particular state or even the principle that there should be a state to, as William Ernest Hocking said, "hinder hindrances."

But if one accepts the evil inherent in the self, it gives the state an intelligible ground. The state is inherently defective, having to use the methods of the opponents of virtue to protect its exercise. It is a part of civilization that would not exist in a perfected civilization, which would be a domain of self-controlled and loving artists. The more the state is needed, the less it is able to fulfill its proper function well: it only appears beneficent when voluntary solidarity or tradition provides social restraint.

The artistry of statecraft is brought to perfection by a leader who is willing to assume responsibility for protecting a group of people. Protopolitical activity is present throughout social life whenever someone takes charge of a conjoint activity and apportions tasks within it. Sometimes the leader's decisions are honored because they aid in the effective accomplishment of that activity, but often they are followed because the leader either appears to be or is confident. Machiavelli was correct in identifying political artistry with *virtù*, the resolve to do what is necessary to bring peace to a community. The civilized leader seeks a virile peace, one in which individuals use the facilities of the civilization to the greatest extent and with the greatest initiative and artistry, and do not destroy the basis for their continued use. Such a leader would seek to allow the maximum diversity of activity within the society, but would curb those activities impelled by destructive impulses or those with destructive consequences, whether or not intended. A combination of permissiveness with resolution—a permissive resolve and a resolute permissiveness—could only be based on the leader's self-limitation to the function of protector and rejection of the temptations to become a creator of civilization or a savior of society. A protector must be confident enough to be comfortable with the sword, yet also reluctant to use it, which involves mastery of hatred and excess, and, most important, control over fear. Discomfort with the sword leads either to a collapse of resolution and a supine permissiveness, or to a resort to terror and rigid despotism to ward off that discomfort. The specific virtue of the leader is cool-headedness, the forebearance from panic, which opens the way to the ability to make adequate decisions in an atmosphere of danger and confusion. The ideal protector pursues the purpose of accustoming people to live with each other in spontaneous and voluntary solidarity by preserving a public space for them to do so.

All arts are reflective, in the sense that they involve a mixing of mind and material that displays design—that is, meaning or purposive order—and that must be attended by consciousness during at least some phase of its exercise, and also attended by some knowledge of that exercise as an art requiring artistry: technical proficiency and, at its fullest development, virtuosity. However much any other art is confounded with religion, which is the art of propitiation, it has its own reflexivity, because the exercise of an art requires care, if not to monitor results then to allow an act to unfold spontaneously, as in the arts associated with Zen Buddhism. Preliterate societies are correctly called sacred in the sense that they surround many of the activities that occur within them and that constitute them with ritual, which is meant to satisfy the forces that control human destiny by adopting a certain style. Ritual contains much of the Freudian compromise formation and of sublimation: threats and wishes are enacted in symbolic form, just as Freud hypothesized in his early essay on the analogy between religion and obsessive-compulsive neurosis. The separation of the arts from a religious cocoon, which is associated with social differentiation, makes their reflexivity stand out, but in the first instance only because the reflexivity of the religious art of propitiation no longer covers it. However, disengagement from religion is only one of the steps necessary to bring an art to full reflexivity. Another step is self-conscious reflection on the meaning of its perfection as an art and on the ways that perfection might be achieved. Self-conscious clarification and criticism characterize the practice of properly reflexive arts, which means that their precise purposes can change in conjunction with improvement in the means they deploy, making possible what is called "progress." Any art is capable of becoming properly reflexive, but the fundamental arts and the art of politics in the first instance are not so. There are, however, arts that are properly reflexive from their inception—that is, their practice requires the attempt to make explicit and pertinent those standards regulating that practice. The three great branches of art in which proper reflexivity is inherent are technology/science, fine art, and philosophy.

The term "technology/science" refers to that branch of the arts concerned with the determination of change according to general rules of transformation of processes. The interpretation of science and technology suggested here takes contemporary Western science as its standard and follows the line advanced by Charles Sanders Peirce and John Dewey. Peirce's contribution to the philosophy of science was to stress its experimental aspect, the submission of an hypothesis to an appropriate test. He noted that the laboratory was an essential component of modern science devoted to shaping material in such a way that it would fit the conditions specified in hypotheses, which means that at least in part a science is a procedure for producing results that conform to a design, but which, if they do not conform, impel an effort to devise a better design. The case is not different for technology, in which a process for achieving a specific result is developed and then tested to determine its reliability. In contemporary society science and technology are nearly fused with one another, the first providing the general description of changes that are then made concrete in the application of a tool. Science here dominates technology, providing designers with the ability to project possible directed changes in advance of a more substantial actualization. The more primal relation, however, is in the other direction, in which science is subordinate, if not to technology, then to technique. John Dewey and Josiah Royce argued that the sciences developed through the abstraction of the operational elements from what have here been called the "fundamental arts." Technique is a way of procuring the transformation of some material to fit a design of the mind. It is possible to study how the transformation itself occurs as the technique is applied and with a sufficient capability for abstraction to measure it in terms of units that symbolize experienced qualities. Science escapes from technique at the point at which it studies changes outside the context of a specific practical art, treating those changes as though they evinced a design, and then trying to discover the details of that design. A further step of separation is taken when units of measurement no longer always refer to observed qualities but to operations that are assumed to occur in order to produce a certain effect. Idealization has permitted some sciences to abstract even from what Santayana called the "pictorial space and sentimental time" of our personal existence. Such daring and flexible use of the concept removes any fetishism from it, showing that science is an art and not a copy of reality, though it is destined to refer to the realities rooted in personal existence.

Samuel Alexander taught that all of the arts involve an "unpiecing" and a "repiecing" of aspects of experience. This process is especially conspicuous in the sciences, in which the qualitative changes that occur through momentary experiences are analyzed into various elements related according to mathematical functions. Science takes the lead over technique due to its embrace of an abstraction disciplined by experimental test but not subservient to any specific effect. Yet it not only depends in great part upon other arts for preformed material, but also uses many of those other arts, particularly those involved with industry, for its experiments. Science provides a description of how things happen, and technique makes things happen. Technology is a synthesis of science and technique that incorporates knowledge of how changes occur into ways of making them occur. Science, therefore, has two distinct functions within a civilization based on the affirmation of life. The first is to provide the knowledge necessary for developing technologies that will extend and expand the capacity for fulfilling those human desires that are consistent with a virtuous life. Here science is only autonomous formally through its interest in calculating changes, but not in terms of its purpose, which belongs to technology. The second function of science is its own, which is to provide a description of the processes of experience that is based on thought disciplined by actual perception. Science does not present its own interpretation of existence as a whole (there is no synoptic science that coordinates all the special sciences), but it does, through each of its branches, acquaint its practitioners with the realities rooted in life in terms of provisional mental constructions. The artistry of science, therefore, involves not only the virtuosity of the craftsperson, the technician, and the engineer, but also a freedom of mind to entertain alternative descriptions of change. As Peirce insisted, science's constitutive rejection of any fixed system of thought means that those of its practitioners who are clear about what their activity involves are delivered to particular lines of inquiry but detached from any tenacious beliefs in the adequacy of those approaches.

Science abstracts from richly variegated momentary experiences the different processes of transformation that occur through and between them, and, as Peirce taught, interprets these processes most generally according to the principle of continuity, what he called "synechism." For science, however, continuity always remains abstract, because the processual aspects of experienced events do not exhaust those events, the qualitative element of experience being discrete, even to the very feeling of constancy. The sciences attempt to measure changes by conceiving of them in terms of homogeneous units that can vary according to quantity. The goal of a science is reached when the transformations it studies can be adequately interpreted in terms of continuous mathematical functions. This goal has not been achieved by any science up to the present, but it is regulative over scientific practice. The kind of world picture that the sciences, taken together, present is one of disjoint schemes of interpretation, each focusing on a part of the concrete. The illusion of scientific completeness arises when one is thinking within a particular scientific theory and mistakes its generality for comprehensiveness, forgetting the restricted scope of data on which it is based. A science is individuated through a theory that describes how certain things happen, not through any specific observations or experiments. The theory itself may have mathematical elegance and attract one to it as a world unto itself. In such a case the theory has passed over from science into fine art, in which it is no longer the "how" of things that matters but what they are in themselves. The fine arts primordially are those spheres of activity in which an effort is made to combine certain particular experiences of the substantial self so that an autonomous or self-satisfying world of experience is created.

Through a creative act of the personal existent, the fine arts, such as painting, literature, music, and cinema, are ways in which the mind interpenetrates a material—here one should say a medium—to produce an object significant unto or for itself. Each fine art is differentiated from the others by its medium, which permits an appeal only to certain possibilities of momentary experience, usually excluding some of the senses from its purview and always excluding a great many images and thoughts from its scope of expression. The fine arts do not stand above various momentary experiences, investigating their processes of change, as science does, or their significance, which is philosophy's task; but they do craft objects to be experienced in moments or chains of moments that will arrest an appreciator's attention, draw that attention into them, because of their intrinsic importance, even if that appreciator be only the artist and even if that importance be the significance of triviality. The fine arts allow momentary experience to be engrossing because of the ways in which particular qualities are arrayed in relation to each other—that is, because of their form, or better, their informed content. In fine art the individual is an object, a work drenched with specificity even if, as in literature, much of that specificity must be provided by an appreciator in a reading, or, as in music, by a performance, which need only occur in the auditory imagination. Yet, though it is concrete, the object of fine art can only be enjoyed reflectively, by keeping account of its singularity, its discontinuity from its environment. This means framing it with a penumbra, however thin, of consciousness of its character as art. Attempts by Richard Wagner and many of his spiritual legatees in the cinema to create a total art, one that involves the appreciator completely—or efforts to make the appreciator an improvisor, as in various forms of participatory art—are directed, when most successful, toward heightening the tension between the emotionally responsive substantial self and the reserved, yet accepting, over-ego.

The term fine art does not distinguish between popular arts and what are conventionally deemed to be higher arts. Popular music, for example, has traditions, standards of criticism, and objects that engross creators and appreciators by placing them in worlds of autonomous significance. As opposed to those arts with clienteles of self-conscious appreciators, it is more likely that the popular arts will serve such ends as promoting merchandise and providing stimulus to get through the vicissitudes of life; the popular arts often function as accompaniments to other tasks of living or as supplements for psyches that crave compensations for their defeats, their frustrated desires, and the anxieties they feel. All fine art, of course, is relevant to other aspects of life, growing out of the experiences that occur in certain social contexts and influencing the way in which experiences that succeed appreciative activity will, in Samuel Alexander's terms, be enjoyed. Those arts conventionally judged to be higher in the West are so not because of their specific media, but because they have developed explicit standards for judging works in terms of their intrinsic perfections rather than according to their extrinsic effects. Insofar as popular artists and their appreciators develop an ongoing community of criticism, they partake in a more civilized pursuit. That such tendencies to make the popular arts higher have thus far tended to isolate their proponents from the generality of individuals, only indicates the low level of civilization in contemporary societies.

The function of the fine arts in a virtuous life is to make a moment or finite sequence of moments significant in its or their particularity for an appreciator, to make concrete experience congenial for a mind in its more substantial response to existence. To be congenial, an object need not give aesthetic pleasure or evince beauty, in the sense of harmonious proportion, though each of these is evidence that the self has discerned significance; it may disturb, arrest, or even confuse. What is necessary is that the work involve the appreciator in a response to it through its own characteristics of in-formed qualities. For art to fulfill its function the appreciator must let the work guide the response without allowing that response to become so ecstatic that the object becomes an extension of the "me," as it does when art is used as an incitement to Dionysian ecstasy. The requirements for the appreciator are similar to those of the artist, whose special virtue is to give the substantial self over to the creation of a complex of in-formed quality, which is a finite expression of finite life, while remaining aware of the integrity of the object being created—that is, careful of its unity as it unfolds. In entering into the fine arts one crosses a bridge between those arts that are more narrowly practical, in the sense of ministering to the satisfaction of desires (that is, in having their significance outside themselves), and those arts that intrinsically perfect the moments of experience by constituting those moments. Although every art may be practiced as a fulfillment of momentary experience, the fine arts and philosophy are constituted so as to be enjoyed for the intrinsic perfection of their objects, not for what these objects can do to actualize ulterior aims or designs.

Fine art is distinguished from philosophy by its nearness to the substantial self. Each work of art is a response to a specific emotion or complex of emotions in the creator, even those whose purpose is to display the structure of some element of sense perception itself. The composition of a song is paradigmatic of this characteristic of fine art. Nietzsche, indeed, fancied that the birth of language was through a process of "primal singing" that expressed the molten flow of feeling, image, and percept in the chain of momentary experiences. As I have experienced composing, a song is incited by a particular mood. Sometimes that mood will be expressed first by a musical phrase, sometimes by a lyric, and sometimes by a line uniting lyric and notes. Once a line has been attained the lyrical meaning and the tone and tempo of the music are either established or nearly so. The line is an integrity of words and music that expresses the inciting mood by re-presenting it in terms transmissible to another self or another moment of the composing self. There is an affinity between the more public data of words and sounds, disposed according to rhythm and melody, and the mood out of which they emerge. This affinity or adhesion of the expression to that which incites it accounts for the ability of a song to create an autonomous world in which the self can become lost. That world is built up around the initial line with more or less deliberate manipulation of technical possibilities, including lists of rhymes. As the entire song unfolds the composer must continually monitor music and lyrics to make sure that they are consistent with the central expression, though sometimes that monitoring leads to a decision to change the entire meaning of the song by, for example, introducing a contrasting mood. The perfection of a song is the precise expression of the inciting mood in such a way that it can be evoked in a listener or a performer rather than just understood. The song, therefore, does not take the self above particular emotional responses but into them by purifying and isolating them, yet it surrounds them with the penumbra of self-conscious artistry. A song fails when it is imprecise and tries to express too many conflicting feelings, images, and ideas. Even Poe, who claimed sometimes to write poems in a purely deliberative spirit, strove for precision about a particular experience. Fine art is partial, not comprehensive. Its vision is not universal but particular.

In contrast to fine art, philosophy is comprehensive. Rather than create a particular significance, it attempts to keep all that is most significant wtihin its vision. As a free reflection on the totality of personal existence, philosophy is both the fruit of civilization and its firmest support, the latter because one of its tasks is to clarify what civilization is. Within the scheme of the arts, philosophy is the one that places the others and itself into an order of dignity while defining each one's contribution to a good life. It also limits the pretensions of the arts by making their substantive effects (or products) and their special virtue (artistry) relative to other virtues. Philosophy is directed toward the over-ego, which, when it is sharply discriminated from the substantial self, has the capacity to accept and not be overwhelmed by any of the shows or faces of experience, whether the adverse or the delightful or the ambivalent. The over-ego cannot be frightened by spontaneous fear or seduced by the lust awakened by seductive objects. Its benign

indifference opens up a field in which all of the relations between substantial self and its environing context can appear as
they are, shorn of either wishful or fearful thinking, both of
which generate an anxiety that prevents the in-drawing act of
ensimismamiento. At the height of discrimination the over-ego
is able to observe even the processes of projection that constitute wishful and fearful thinking, just as some dreams are
framed by the bystander's awareness. But then they are no longer
achieved projections. Philosophy's principle is to be true to life,
which means to acknowledge both the radical reality of the
self and the independent, though rooted, reality of that which is
not self. It is only through the discrimination of over-ego from
substantial self that self, world, and other self become clearly
demarcated.

Whereas the fine arts are primarily tied to the process of
expression, philosophy is reflective. The interpenetration of mind
and material in the philosophical object is established by the
declaration-proposition "my life is the radical reality" through
which the substantial aspects of life are displayed to a center
of awareness and thereby given the form of being the perspective
of that center: the act of self-possession creates the domain
in which the art of philosophy can be practiced, but it is not
philosophy itself, which must hold fast to self-possession in
order to discover what is significant to the free self. The work
of philosophy is, as Socrates understood, a life that has been
examined and has become lucid to itself, which involves
knowledge of the pervasive characteristics of that life and, after
reflective review, of the most important kinds of things within
it. Philosophers, however, are not autobiographers who express
the particularities of their lives, but are investigators of personal existence who explore the only domains to which they
have access, their own. A philosopher offers an invitation to con-
ceive of and judge personal existence in a certain way. The
offer is made in some form such as, "See if you don't assent to

these descriptions and evaluations of life once you have attempted to understand your own life in their terms." A philosophy communicates the results of and the methods used in an
examination of life as candidly and, for the most part—inasmuch as concrete examples often are expedient—as generally as
possible. To appreciate a communicated work of philosophical
art, one must install oneself within the vision of existence presented by the philosopher and find out whether and, if so,
how that vision has made one more coincident with or at home
with oneself, able to better comprehend a totality in terms of the
just proportion of its significant elements, where justice and
significance are relative to the free valuation of the philosophizing self.

The philosopher's artistry is similar to that of the fine artist,
but on the plane of reflection, not of expression. Just as the
fine artist must be delivered to a particular response of the substantial self and yet attend to the unity of that response, the
philosopher must give informed and candid descriptions and
evaluations of each phase of personal existence while being
aware of the other phases and the way they should limit the re-
port of the aspect under consideration. Control over the parts
in philosophy has traditionally been achieved by systematization,
in which certain highly general principles provide a coherence
to which more particular discussions can be assimilated, either
by an attempt at demonstrating connection in terms of formal
logic or in terms of analogy. There must be some systematization in philosophy or it would not offer an interpretation of
personal existence as a whole. But it should not reach the point
at which it forecloses fresh and independent reflection on the
various phases of experience: the philosopher should no more
dogmatize a system than a scientist should dogmatize a theory.
However, philosophy differs from science in that an independent
reflection that seems to clash with certain general principles
need not generate a new system but may only introduce paradox

into it. The aim of philosophy is not self-consistent descriptions and evaluations, but those that are adequate and true to life, which truth sometimes involves one in contradictory statements. The artistry of philosophy involves maintaining a balance between unfolding system and independent insight—sensing when a specific description or evaluation is becoming distorted because the descriptions and evaluations that limit it are being ignored or suppressed—and when an independent insight that is counterposed to other understandings should stand as a paradox. There is no standard but free, comprehensive, and reflective valuation to guide one in achieving that balance.

The arts that compose civilization contain their own perfection and virtue in their practice and, for the most part, produce objects that satisfy desires and/or palliate fears. Though satisfaction does not belong within the realm of virtue, which is one of agency, it is essential to the good life, not only because many satisfactions refer to the fulfillment of requirements for continued vitality, but also because the pleasure that suffuses a satisfaction itself enhances the affirmation of life that makes possible the practice of virtue, which involves prolonged effort. The fundamental arts, the art of leadership, and science/technology clearly produce results meant to fulfill desires. The objects of fine art and philosophy create autonomous realms of value that engender the desire for them when they are experienced. The artistry of an art is subordinate to the kind of mixture of mind and material appropriate to its object, and beyond that to the desire it is supposed to satisfy and to the feeling that accompanies the fulfillment of that desire. The preceding formulation is not meant to suggest what is often called "psychologism"—the doctrine that the validity of knowledge and of valuation is grounded in states of the psyche—but to adumbrate the intelligible structure of artistic activity. This structure must always be proximally referent to its object and more distantly related to its background in feeling and impulse, and, in the direction of the over-ego, to the artistry of its performance. The concern to minister to the fulfillment of desire is not a topic properly discussed under the head of the virtue of artistry, but is correctly treated under that of love. Artistry is concerned first for the proximate object and then, most virtuously, for itself. Its practice embodies a confidence that the appreciator—whose requirements have, for the moment, been assumed to have been expressed in the specifications of an object—will be satisfied by a good work. There are, of course, certain arts such as medicine, teaching, and politics in which artistry incorporates an element of love, because the objects of such arts are intimately implicated with other selves. Yet even in these arts there is an element of ruthless attention to objectivity that if not checked can lose sight of the particular individual who is patient. The art of philosophy is, perhaps, the most ruthless one of all because it is the most detached from the whirl of the feelings and desires of the substantial self. It is meant to present a set of judgments as candidly and precisely as possible regardless of any ulterior effect on the philosopher or anyone else. Its confidence in doing so is based on the affirmation of life which, the more reflective it becomes, issues in benign detachment.

The separation of artistry from the other aspects of artistic activity—that is, the pursuit of art for its own sake—is both the crown and the support of the arts. Care for the perfection of performance is what keeps the arts in good form, and if they are not in good form, not practiced virtuously, they fail and are less than arts, which are inherently aristocratic even when their practice and appreciation are widespread. The art of automotive repair, for example, fails when the machine is more damaged by efforts to fix it than it was when it broke down. Cooking similarly fails when the food is unpalatable—for example, when the ingredients are improperly proportioned, not cleaned thoroughly, contain impurities, or are over- or underdone. Competence and concern are combined in artistry in the service of an object's perfection. But as familiarity with an art grows, the object may begin to recede from the forefront of attention and the practice itself become engrossing because it has been perfected enough to guarantee the production of a successful object. The arts associated with Zen Buddhism carry to its completion this kind of separation of artistry from the other phases of artistic activity and thereby evince that virtue. As Eugen Herrigel describes it, the art of archery, when practicad as a discipline of Zen, is brought to fulfillment when the body spontaneously, indeed effortlessly, performs the acts of drawing and shooting without any anxious strain toward the target, yet the arrow hits the center of the target just because the activity has been consummated with such grace and fluidity. Herrigel describes the principle of the experience of a perfected Zen art as "actionless action." That paradox refers to the condition of performing an act without consciousness of the object that one will produce, yet with ease and freedom that concretely display confidence and competence, and are earnests of success. Practice of a Zen art is a continual clearing away of anxious anticipation, either as desire or fear, so that artistry can become self-sufficient for a moment. There may even come an instant at which performance becomes so free and easy that attention is drawn away from the exercise of the virtue of artistry itself and into a domain of vivid calm in which the participation of the self in constituting momentary experience is encased within its qualitative whole and observed benignly. At such instants the Zen arts approximate the art of sitting and step beyond civilization per se, serving as steppingstones to the discrimination of knower from field.

The Zen arts achieve the result of separating over-ego from substantial self by training the latter to perfect a performance, by delivering it to that performance, and not by diminishing the significance of artistry as certain ascetic tendencies do. Zen is an embrace of participation in life through art that leads by

way of its success to artlessness, spontaneity. The fulfillment
of Zen experience restricts the arts most appropriate to it to
those whose performance may be contained within a single
momentary experience. For example, a perfected haiku is supposed to be composed within the tract of time bounded by the
experience of a breath: as one breathes in one is supposed
to drink in a scene, and as one exhales one is supposed to express
it in seventeen syllables. The poem, therefore, must unfold without forethought and deliberation, its artistry must be inherent
in spontaneous expression and prescind from reflection altogether, yet it must be adequate to what is seen, not to images
that occur to the self, as in free association. Haiku is a discipline
that draws the self out into its context of orientation, which it
then must learn to express for its own sake in precise and
subtly evocative words: it is a taming of expression, a subordi-
nating of it to concrete actuality, which transmits the nub of
that actuality to another moment. But the more successful the
discipline of haiku is in drawing the self out into its context and
assimilating expression to it, the more the over-ego is freed to
observe the entire happening, which need not—indeed, cannot—be cared for or tended. As soon as an attempt is made to
care for it, the spontaneity dissolves and the haiku is not
achieved. There may be a poem, even a good one, but not an
achieved experience of the perfection of artistry, which passes
beyond art to contemplation, as it takes art along with it. All
of the arts associated with Zen Buddhism have the same structure and finality as haiku poetry, incorporating rigorous and
prolonged discipline to perfect a performance sufficiently to release the over-ego from any need to monitor the substantial self.
The few such moments so attained are for the traditional
practitioner of a Zen art a raison d'être.

One of the arts most appropriate to educing the range of experiences associated with Zen is that of sitting, discussed in the

preceding chapter as a method of achieving and evincing self-control. Here the object is the body and the substantial self, the limbs being disposed in a way to maximize the stability of the body so that the feelings and moods of the psyche stand out as interior to the self and relative to a wider field. In a deep meditation the images and expressive responses of the substantial self are allowed free play, but no release into muscular activity. There may come a time in such meditative activity that the substantial ego seems to lapse from view altogether. There is an awareness of an absence of any specific mood, of what might be called an opening in the area usually dominated by the substantial self, leaving the over-ego observing a body that has been tranquilized not by relaxation but by a complex system of counterbalancing muscular tensions. This, I take it, is what commentators such as D. T. Suzuki mean when they speak of the Zen doctrine of "no mind." Sitting is such a special activity for some Zen teachers because the practice of this art is so congenial to the achievement of "no mind." In other arts the trained spontaneity of the performance may be perfected enough to permit the over-ego to be freed from its monitoring function. However, even in such cases the substantial ego is not effaced but is in a fully harmonious interaction or better, as John Dewey and Arthur Bentley had it, transaction with the material-in-formation. In sitting, the substantial ego is cut off from deliverance into the self's context of orientation and is left to thrash around on its own account until all of the body's tendencies for calm become strong enough to limit its pre-tensions: fears and desires take on the guise of pre-tensions, of images accompanied by feelings of strain, and thereby are given a boundary within the self's momentary experience or actuality. The way in which a body properly disposed by sitting is enjoyed is by allowing the substantial self to dissipate so that no mind is left to be intermediary between over-ego and what can only be thought of as pure perception or, in other terms, as the intuition of an essence.

The "opening" created by a perfected session of meditation or by the practice of some other art in the Zen way of directing artistry toward the liberation of the over-ego indicates some of the general conditions for the exercise of artistic virtue. In sitting, the resistance that must be overcome primarily is that of the "me," the assertive ego, which is most clearly evinced when one is "full of oneself." One sits down initially with a relatively unruly "me," made so in part by the need to mobilize it in order to get the activity started. Indeed, the practice of any art, even when one is an expert at it, is haunted by the resistance to exert effort, take trouble, suffer regimentation. There is no more effective and easy immediate incentive to initiating some artistic activity than a feeling of self-importance that reflects back to make the activity significant, though it pretends that it is justified in terms of the activity's importance. Once the artistic endeavor has begun, however, self-feeling becomes a hindrance to perfection, because it turns attention away from the unfolding object and toward the "me," adding to artistry pride in one's exercise of it. The arrogant expert or virtuoso has learned how to combine extreme self-feeling at the inception and conclusion of the activity with strict attention to the perfection of the performance while it is underway. As Herrigel reports, Zen masters do not look kindly upon a successful technical performance of an art that is surrounded by pride. Their anger and contempt, however, reveal Zen's bad secret: that artistry can be cultivated and perfected to a high intensity without spilling over into a more general benignity and detachment. In sitting, however, the very object is discrimination of over-ego from substantial self; thus, the "vital contradiction," as Santayana called such conditions, between assertion of the "me" and the exercise of artistry becomes apparent. One cannot be proud of sitting at a moment in which one is practicing the art or there is no artistry to that practice. All of the other arts are the same in effect, but their concrete practice may be composed of moments of subservience to the ob-

ject interrupted by moments of self-inflation and self-congratu-
lation. Such goads of and to the substantial self only show that
the self involved in the activity must continually recommit
itself to that activity, in a sense constantly to reinitiate it. In
sitting, however, such reinitiation does not prolong the act, but
aborts it, revealing a conflict concealed at the heart of all the
other arts. Sitting cultivates a distinction between pride and confidence, the former being an attempt to keep up morale by
restricting the substantial self to a will to believe, and the
latter betokening a trust in the substantial self's spontaneity
or at least a willingness to risk such a trust.

The Zen arts are a schooling in confidence because they combine the persistent discipline that Nietzsche thought necessary
to enhance the feeling of power with the Taoist principle of
wei-wu-wei or "doing nothingness." Zen, indeed, might be
thought of as Taoism in a civilized key, as a group of regimens
for making oneself fit to let-be, to deliver oneself into one's
context of orientation without collapsing the distance between
over-ego and substantial self. Zen differs from Taoism in exalting
art as a steppingstone to liberation rather than in eschewing
it for a more primal ease. The Zen way is not that of abandonment to one's context of orientation but of direction toward
integral participation in that context through the creation of a
perfected work of art. Although small fine arts such as flower
arranging, haiku, and brush-stroke painting are most congenial
to Zen, any art may be practiced in a Zen spirit. For example,
the art of driving that was discussed earlier is perfected under
dangerous conditions by "doing nothingness." When one
drives an ice-covered road one must allow the car to skid
slightly and not try to prevent it from going off the road by
turning the steering wheel too precipitously or slamming on
the brakes. To drive with such artistry, however, one must trust
one's substantial self not to panic and to have trained one's re-
flexes to respond subtly; that is, one can only let be when one

has become sufficiently competent to feel that the machine is an extension of one's body and that the responses of the body are under one's control. For Zen the perfection of life lies through art and then beyond it.

The perfection of the practice of an art brings momentary experience to a fulfillment by building it into a coherent form. The activity of the self appears to coincide with that upon which the self operates so that the experience becomes an initiative rather than a response that is distant or detached from its stimulus. Practice of the Zen arts or of arts in the Zen spirit makes possible the idea of a life that at least in one of its aspects is making each momentary experience, in the sense of the lived present, an initiative. Of course it is never really possible to do this because the substantial self never comes up empty-handed but is, rather, clotted with sense and feeling that it then struggles to express. We are basically receivers and not givers; what we give is in terms of what we have received. This is a mark of finitude even more certain than death: if there is a Being, the essence of which is to exist, it is surely not the personal existent possessing a life in which "rooted realities" are obtrusive. Nonetheless the attempt can be made to cut to the smallest margin the response time necessary to turn a lived present into an initiative. Whenever one is "doing something," that is, practicing an art, the successive phases of each particular chain of moments flow along as an activity, the material being shaped with freedom and ease unless an obstacle is encountered, in which case the basic responsiveness of the self is evidenced. In moments during which one is not engrossed in the practice of an art, however, the artistry of perfecting the moment requires an alertness to the significance of what the self receives so that it will be able to "rise to the occasion"; that is, it must be able to discern what dimension of the data are important enough to be emphasized in the response and which data should be muted. The cultivation of such alertness can be illustrated by the Zen story of the disciple whose master trained him in the art of swordsmanship by employing him as a cook and then assaulted him continually with pots, pans, and other utensils. He had to be ready to practice the art of cooking and in a split second transform that art into one of self-defense. He had to recognize that experience can always surprise, that any form is vulnerable to invasion from that which is alien to itself, yet he had to make the surprise into an initiative. As a way of living, Zen means binding oneself into actuality as a transforming participant. As noted above, that participation may become so coherent that contemplation supervenes over the purest activity. And is the purest activity the haiku or the brush-stroke painting? They come close to Heidegger's idea of a response of thanksgiving to Being.

The preceding remarks left open the question of how one can determine what kind of participation is appropriate to a moment. If one is to catch each emerging moment on the fly, it is not possible to sit back in a judgmental posture and deliberate about one's response to it; that is, the response cannot be determined fully by the application of any intellectual principle. One must, as Aristotle taught, become habituated to virtue, which means deliberating wholeheartedly in some moments about what is good and what one's duties are, but also training oneself to embody one's free valuations of significance in the more primal responses of the substantial self. Beyond any particular habits, however, is a spirit of living into a moment that arises from the affirmation of life. Zen literature is filled with the steady and confident joy, so different from Dionysian ecstasy, of the embrace of momentary experience, of being-in-act. But the import of rising to the occasion is, I think, most precisely defined in Hasidic Judaism, at least as Martin Buber expounds it. The core of the peaceful yet mirthful joy that colors a fulfilled Hasidic life is the disposition to "release the Shekinah," that is, the spark of divinity—

in terms of this work one would think of it as the perfection—
that each situation contains. The participation of the Hasidic
Jew in momentary experience is governed not by the demands of
the "me" or—which is most often the case in everyday life—of
the "me" in conjunction with another of the self's personae, but
by the total context of orientation as a field for bringing to
actuality a fullness of time, a perfected present. Although the
spirits of Zen Buddhism and Hasidic Judaism are compatible and
lead to many of the same experiences, Zen takes the side of
the loving warrior, whereas Hasidism favors the lover and,
thereby, tends in a Dionysian direction. One is guided by the
Hasidic view of things to seek what is precious in each moment,
what should be brought out of it to make goodness show forth.
That special concern places a significance on adverse or merely
uninspiring experiences that is not as great in Zen and is often
absent in contemporary everyday life, though it pervades the
fundamental arts. The French housekeeper treats her cooking in
a Hasidic spirit, buying common ingredients and transforming
them into delightful dishes. Indeed, the fundamental art of
cooking, wherever it is practiced with artistry by a wide range of
a population, is a way of "releasing the Shekinah." Zen and
Hasidism are both necessary to a life permeated by artistry, that
is, to an artistic sense of life. Zen provides the opening, through
its cultivation of trained spontaneity and alertness, for a deliverance to the particular perfection to which one's unreserved
participation in a situation can contribute.

Zen and Hasidism are markedly unsentimental, calling for
strict attention to the fulfillment of each actuality. In the modern
life of the middle class, which is ramified in a multitude of directions and parceled out into highly specialized and widely
diverse contexts of orientation, such unreserved deliverance to
the moment requires an ability to deploy, nearly spontaneously,
a broad repertoire of personae, each tailored to the social setting
in which one is involved. One must be able to move from one

social space to the next, shedding immediately the mental
garments one had just been sporting and changing into new ones.
Living this way, social norms become provisional and utterly
relative to the particularity of one's immediate context. That context includes other people. It is a temptation of one who attempts to make of the moments of life excuses for artistry to
interpret other selves as participants in a drama that one is
creating on the spur of the moment. Here artistry reaches a limit
and descends into delusion, not through fear, but through excess,
and can only be redeemed by love, which treats the other self
not as material to be in-formed by a mind that penetrates it (the
way of political leadership and statecraft), but as an independent
and spontaneous center of conscious experience and expression.
One may, of course, broaden Zen and Hasidism to include a
disposition to love; and particularly in the case of the latter,
that addition would be historically accurate. But the essence of
love is not artistry, even when it is evinced most tenderly. Love,
indeed, is the highest form of releasing the Shekinah, because it is
the bringing forth of the fullness of the other self. But that
activity of "educing," to use Coleridge's term, does not involve
living-into a moment, taking materiality up into activity. Instead it is primarily involved in clearing tracts of space and time
for the other to participate wholeheartedly in the life of virtue.
In love one makes an impress upon the other self, but only by
submitting to the impress of the other upon oneself, what
Unamuno called "mutual imposition." Love, then, involves a
surrender of artistry at many strategic moments, but the self that
has felt the artistic sense of life finds its stressful pleasures
uniquely precious.

The virtue of the self toward itself is self-control, and that of the self toward the objects in its context of orientation (including its imaginations and thoughts) is artistry. Self-control is essentially an acceptance, a letting-be, a profound tolerance of all that is given. Artistry, which is founded upon self-control, is a rejection of what is given in terms of a model—which in a creative act unfolds as the artistry proceeds—that guides a transformative process. John Dewey, who tended to give artistry even more than its due, discussed self-control under the heading of "arts of acceptance," and artistry under that of "arts of control." Dewey often believed that science, the most refined art of control, would make possible a diminished need for practicing the arts of acceptance. He did not realize that many of the children of leisure (and they began appearing with frequency in the first half of the nineteenth century) would discover that nothing could redeem the decay of their bodies. The rebellion against the adverse aspects of existence is the black hole into which all of life is sucked in Dostoevsky's thought. Dostoevsky, of course, was not entirely pleased with this rebellion, which was intrinsic to his very self-definition, and counterposed to it Father Zossima's

vision of paradise (the parallels to Hasidism should be noted)
and Alyosha's deceptively simple-minded kindness. Is there
another way to handle the "sickness unto death" in its most concrete form of horror of the flesh? The underground man is so
spiteful that he won't even take care of his liver, the only reliable
defense against most toxins. Dewey would think this sort of
behavior childish, and there is no doubt that it is. But who is
not a child? What does it take to be a man? (By man I mean
one who is self-possessed, who can say, and accept the consequences of saying, "My life is the radical reality." I should say
man or independent woman. Or must a woman become a man in
order to be independent?) I am not satisfied with Dewey's sort
of manhood, which amounts—if it does not turn out (as I think
it does) to be based on the arts of acceptance—to losing oneself
in a cause to which one's skin and attention can adhere. Or is
Dewey more a hedonist than a Calvinist, looking toward the
consummations provided by the arts rather than their perfection.
He sometimes seems so in *Art as Experience*. But primarily he
wants a balance between the two spirits. What can we do with
this quintessential American philosopher, so eclectic, so reason-
able, so willing to deceive himself? Bring him back to the flesh
where he claimed he began.

Perhaps there *are* people who have criticized every abstract
idea that was helping them to live and have then settled back
peacefully to watch their bodies deteriorate, intervening more or
less frequently in the affairs of their contexts to make them more
congenial to life. I find that difficult, though certainly not impossible, to believe. Such individuals would have transmuted
tolerance into joy, acceptance into complete affirmation. This
kind of vision, I think, lies behind Nietzsche's idea of the over-
man, someone who affirms life as it is, who lives in joyful sight
of the truth. Nietzsche is still the heir of Beethoven, who trans-
figured Schiller's "Ode to Joy"; he could not give up the wish,
though his vision was of the abyss. Nietzsche remained a romantic, though he could not lead the romantic's life. But, of

course, he was much more than that. He, like Dostoevsky, was
close to the flesh and at his most lucid and civilized, as in *Daybreak,* elaborated a psychology based on strict attention to the
shifting feelings and moods of the substantial self in response to
cycles of nature expressed in the body. The over-man, in any
case, did not exist but needed to be created. In *Daybreak* there is
almost no romanticism, in the sense of self-conscious aesthetic
compensation for the failings of life. Instead the "arts of acceptance" are defended in their purest form, their fruit being an
enhanced "sense of power." Here the "sense of power" fills the
role later played by the dogmatic idea of a "will to power,"
which ignores the desire to give way. The "sense of power" is a
mood of confidence, a vital sense of being concretely in control
of one's responses to the realities rooted in one's life. To possess
it means to feel firmly implanted in the world, resistant to adversity, yet able to have one's consciousness englobe the body
and the particular expressions of the self, and to place them in
the same perspective as the rooted realities. The ability to exist
alongside and above one's experience is gained through exercise
of the virtue of self-control and of the "arts of acceptance" that
fortify it, such as psychoanalysis and meditation. Manliness in
this case means complete tolerance of oneself and, when that
fails, tolerance of one's intolerance. It means essentially being
able to be alone with oneself, not merely out of direct contact
with others but actually having no mediate occupation with
them by, for example, doing a favor, writing a letter, performing
part of a cooperative task, planning how one will behave in a
future encounter, or picking over a past occasion. Self-control
meets adversity by stressing the personal character of existence,
its solitude, not in order to clear a space for God or for Being,
but to allow the self to become coincident with itself. Once
abstract ideas no longer guide one's life, it all comes down to
either playing the underground man or to toughening oneself
to adversity.

The toughening process has very strict limits, the sense of

power being a highly variable mood that is continually subject to
dissipation. Self-control must ever be renewed by its exercise, its
place in this discussion paralleling that of authentic repetition
in the thought of Kierkegaard and Heidegger. Renewal, however, is inconstant, and the child usually dominates the man. Did
Dewey not have to contend with childish rebellion, did he
repress it, or was he adept at genuine self-control, perhaps so
much so that he failed to notice its importance? Depression,
suffering, and fear were certainly familiar to him, and it appears
that he often did not fend them off with a will to believe; yet his
struggles found no place in his public writings. America's
premier public philosopher made things seem easier than they
were, probably much easier than they actually were for him.
Part of the aim of the present discussion is to correct what I con-
ceive to be an American delusion that life can be made comfortable. In the first place the arts that bring comfort depend on
artistry which, in turn, cannot be exercised in the absence of
self-control. Anyone who doubts that should read E. M. Forster's
"The Machine Stops," which presents a compelling vision of the
breakdown of an automated society in which human beings are
isolated recipients of the products of an industrial process and
are unable to care for themselves and surely not for each other.
Second, and more important, the best that art can do to dispel
suffering is to palliate it, which means that some way must still
be found to endure it—that is, unless one decides not to endure
it, an option that a foolishly romantic Camus tried to discredit.
The kind of clearheaded person who could lead one of Camus's
absurd lives could defend that life only by pointing out what
made it worth living. When self-control fails there is no call for
disapproval. The fundamental virtue is self-control, and the arts
of acceptance always have the last word in a virtuous life,
though they are not its fulfillment. The deliberate transformation
of the context of orientation through the arts builds upon self-
control and cannot be sustained without it. But the arts do not

only depend upon the support of self-control—that is, are perfected by the self—but their products and practice are for selves. They are oriented in the virtue of love.

It is, perhaps, surprising that a chapter about love should be introduced by such stern words as the preceding ones. In fact, it hadn't occurred to me to take up such a sobering stance until I sat down to write, and the thought of death, disease, and decay began to impose itself on me. There can be no doubt that the philosophically inclined mind tends toward the founding act of philosophy, the declaration of one's own radical reality, which declaration helps to create that reality by bringing it to a greater completion, what in Whitehead's terms would be a higher grade of experience. Self-possession carries with itself separation of the self from that which is not itself. And in that little domain that the self owns, a sense of time sneaks in that finally permeates its whole structure when the awareness of finitude and its signs becomes acute. Philosophy cannot be separated from acknowledgment of being-toward-death. My life is that of a man of flesh and bone, and if I forget that, there is always pain to remind me. Not that I'm getting older and am more subject to pain. I am sure that I have always ached all over but just did not attend to my feelings because I was so wrapped up in chasing after some idea or image. Pain is a station on the way to death; it is a smoldering presence in the body that when it flares up threatens to overwhelm. It is always there, but for many people the threat is distant. Philosophy is not simply an abstract business. As Sartre said, it "carries through" a thought, that is, applies it over the fullest range to which it is applicable. The thought in the case of the present work is that of radical separation. When carried through, this thought has led me—up to now—to both the personal character of embodied existence and the inescapable distinction between knower and field. When I declare myself to be the radical reality, I may either be drawn toward the body and through it into the rooted realities, or toward an awareness ever more distant from even the promptings of expression and thought. The first direction is my inescapable destiny; it gives me the concreteness of my life. It is here where I learn to agonize over death, disease, and decay, and, yes, to pity myself. Indeed, I find self-pity one of the least offensive manifestations of the "me"; it can sometimes issue in a more generalized compassion, which is the surest emotional foundation for love. The second direction, toward discrimination of over-ego from substantial self, involves a kind of acrobatics, a wonderful expedient for perfecting things that is the inherent facilitator of virtue and, thus, the fundamental virtue. It must be cultivated for its own sake— for its inherent benignity—for the resistance it allows to adversity (it is the only resistance available to a self-possessed life), and for the clearing it provides for the virtues of artistry and love. But, as is all virtue, it is an expedient, a way of perfecting life in its very exercise.

The philosopher who has become habituated to radical separation must find his way to love, which in many ways seems contradictory to such separation. A solitary judge of life cannot sacrifice his independence and, so, cannot love in such a way as to take the judgments of another person as any more than advice and counsel. The foundation of a philosopher's love will be separation, not union; love will be a joining of the disparate into a fragile solidarity, but that solidarity will never be tight enough to permit the surrender of self-possession. As a virtue, a perfection of life, love may be made possible by the spontaneous attraction exerted by another self, but it must transmute the element of relatively passive response into committed activity. Love, conceived of as a virtue, does not befall a person, but takes over a desire to possess and to be possessed, and transforms it into a will to serve. I am decidedly not saying here that love is a sublimation of or a reaction formation against any sexual impulses. One of the chief ways in which love serves personal existence is sexually; it makes sexual activity into a way of cherishing the other's body by giving it a special pleasure. The reciprocity of sexual love lies in the fact that the more pleasure one is given, the more pleasure one feels like giving—the impulses that support love being nourished by it, and love being enhanced by those impulses. Love does not substitute for sexual play, but perfects it by orienting it toward the other's inward satisfaction, leaving one's own satisfaction in the other's care: each one gives one's own body over to the other without surrendering the distance necessary to care for the other and to attend to the other's responses. Love, then, is intrinsically neither carnal nor adverse to carnality, but is essentially free service; it issues from the self as its own initiative, as a declaration-deed discontinuous from the feelings that environ it, yet welcomes those feelings and seeks to cultivate them. There is nothing dour about love, though the service involved is often excruciating. Yet it is not reducible to the expansive emotion of sympathy, as Rousseau believed. Love requires sympathy, but it is not determined by it. It transmutes sympathy into devotion, which searches beyond sympathy for elements of the other that are alien to the self, seeking to express them and, if they are deemed valuable when understood, to educe them even more fully. Love is the analogue to artistry in the self's relation to the other self. It is not the same as artistry because love perfects another self, not an object, and the perfection of another self does not involve its conformity to a design, even to one that unfolds within a chain of momentary experiences comprehending a creative act, but requires its liberation to virtue, including its self-possession and, thus, its freedom. The service love performs is to bring out the best in the other, the other's virtue in its unique expression. And it does this in great part by making the other happy in all of the various benign ways it can be done, yet never allowing its service to transform the other into a dependent.

Love, for the one who is habituated to radical separation,

thrives on acknowledging the radical separation of other selves. In its most general sense that acknowledgment is based on the contrast between experiences of communion, which give selves to one another mutually, and those of confinement to actuality, which make the otherness of the other stand out. Communion is the evidence that service is not an empty gesture, that there is someone to serve, but it is transient and sporadic, and it can only enliven love, not sustain it over any extended period of time. Indeed, when they are intense, experiences of communion often result in a resentment against the other when they end and the other is no longer available, no longer willing or able to be entrusted with oneself so fully. Love, as a virtue, would be better understood not as a fruition of communion, though it is that too, but as a way of orienting self toward other that makes communion more characteristic of life and less episodic in its appearance.

From this viewpoint communion is the crown of the life of love, a primary indication that the virtue of love has been exercised. The emotional response that is the greatest enhancer of love is compassion, which is manifest most fully when one identifies oneself with all finite life, especially with personal existence, and merges the failure of one's own body with that of all others. One does not thereby lose the sting of one's own being-toward-death, but rather makes it even more intense by understanding it as part of the general course of things. Such compassion fosters a mood of acceptance of the other as a fellow sufferer that deepens and heightens the actuality of the momentary joys of communion.

Thus far I have discussed love as though its meaning were unequivocal and apparent by its usage. There are, of course, a multitude of meanings for the word "love" and many schemes for classifying love's variants. Here the term is used in a special way to accord with the order of virtues being exposed. Most important, love in the present discussions refers to a way of orienting the self toward other selves, not to a feeling or emotion of the self that signals, helps constitute, and confirms an affirmative response to some rooted reality in or to the radical reality of one's own life. People frequently proclaim their love for their favorite objects or for life itself, meaning, in the first case, either that their enjoyment of the objects satisfies them or that they cherish the objects as they might another person; and in the second, that they are filled with vivacity, that life, for them, is on an upswing. There is none but a terminological problem in using "love" to cover a wide variety of responses to gratifying objects that center around a desire that cares for the integrity of its object, even when it consumes that object. For example, if one claims to "love" candy in this sense, one might be expected to savor particularly candy when one ate it, showing a concern for the specific effects of the object upon oneself. Similarly, to love life means to desire to keep living because one cherishes one's present vital feeling or "sense of power." A more substantial problem arises when love for objects means devotion to them as though they were persons or had some of the basic characteristics of personal existence. Personification of rooted realities is a widespread tendency in human life and is, perhaps, a spontaneous mechanism that must be blocked in modern societies through extensive training in the withdrawal of projections. From the viewpoint of civilized life presented here, treating an object in ways that are appropriate to a personal existent is fetishism. Yet I am not comfortable with taking too hard a judgmental line on this issue. There is a dimension of artistry that draws the practitioner into cherishing the particular tools on which the art depends for its exercise. The fine adjustment to the peculiarities of these tools that is demanded of the artist approaches care for the uniqueness of specific selves. A writer may come to cherish the language, just as a driver may come to care for the integrity of a car. But in such cases there cannot be love in the sense of service because the object is cherished as an extension of oneself, as a vehicle through which an activity is perfected. The case becomes more clear in such examples as a miser's devotion to money. Here the intention is simply to possess, though the result is to be possessed; the miser is symbolic of the failure of love, as is the wastrel, who will not possess in order to avoid being possessed.

Even the broad usage of the term "love" to refer to a desiring that cherishes its object, contains something of love as free service, which at its fruition is not at all oriented toward one's own satisfaction but to the coming-to-be of the other's perfection. Care for an object, however, only extends as far as it gratifies (unless it is a fetish), whereas service to a self is for the freedom of that self, whether or not the lover is satisfied with how that freedom is exercised. The virtue of love as treated here must be distinguished from service to an art. There is a sense that in pursuing an art and in attempting to perfect its practice, one serves that art by allowing one's attention to be fixed on the synthesis of mind and material that is sought, and not on the "me" or on any other persona composing the substantial self. It is only abstractly, however, that one can speak of service to an art, because the art is not in any real way to be differentiated from its exercise and from the appreciation of its products. Unless one believes that there are forms that subsist apart from the creative activity of personal existents and that provide models of artistic perfection, "service" to culture is a figurative usage of the term. The objects formed by the arts are only realized in their creation and appreciation, that is, in their concrete references to the responses of particular selves. The idea of love of art, in the sense of being servitor of a muse—or, in modern times, of a collective endeavor, such as science or some humane tradition—stresses the side of experience of being possessed rather than that of possessing. Giving oneself to an art to the extent of being possessed by it means losing sight of its concrete references both to other arts and to the aspects of personal existence that are foundational to and transcend the purposive transformation of material according to a design. The same sort of considerations apply to such sentiments as love of humanity or of nation. There is a moment in the practice of an art when the practitioner observes the work and, if it is found to be successful, admires it as sufficient unto itself. Subservience to art or to some abstract receptacle for it, such as nation or humanity, takes this moment of fulfillment and makes it a *raison d'être*; it is not love but a way of evading love's risk. One can fail in the exercise of an art, but one cannot be failed by an art. In love the autonomy of the other self opens the possibility that one will be failed.

The above remarks should not be construed to detract from efforts to preserve objects, to care for them, or to contribute, through the arts, to the lives of persons to whom the artist has no direct connection. The important consideration here is that love be referred to other concrete selves, that self-control and artistry be turned toward the cultivation of individuality in others. I stumble here upon a difficulty, or perhaps it is an opportunity, that has not been resolved (or exploited) by the preceding essay in definition: why should love be the crowning virtue? I am haunted, and I must be if I am a reflective lover, by the self-sufficiency of a life based on self-control and artistry. I do not mean by self-sufficiency that I could go it alone, without the help of other selves, that I am not a social being, but that once I have become habituated to the philosophic standpoint, I no longer need to love or to be loved. It is not the same with self-control and artistry: I need them just to survive. And I begin to see that there is an answer to my question in the very problem I pose: part of the perfection of love is its very gratuity, its transcendence over survival needs. Love, just as do self-control and artistry, opens up an entirely new dimension of experience for the self, but it is one that mocks the self in

many ways, rather than enhancing its sense of power as do the
other two virtues. In the other self I reach, as Sartre understood,
an absolute limit on myself, another center of personal existence
whose life is or may be brought to be its own radical reality.
If I dispose myself toward the other in a way that acknowledges
personality, the sense of the other as a "rooted" reality in my
life starts to dissolve and a sense of a far more complete alterity,
indeed, one that is enigmatic, takes its place. But this very
otherness, the gratuity of it to my singular perspective, is what
allows the free service of love truly to be free.

How far does love extend? In modern times the love of God
that transcended loves for particular finite individuals has been
replaced or at least supplemented by love for historical entities
such as country, nation, class, civilization, and the grandest abstraction of all, humanity. How convenient it seems to be to
project one's service into the life of a group; there is a sense of
stability and direction gained from believing that one's contribu-
tions are objective, that they have a resolute meaning which
cannot be overthrown by personal whim, by arbitrary and self-
willed rejection. Such love for the collective, however, is scarcely
love at all, but more a way in which individuals overcome their
loneliness without having to face up to the reality of the other
persons around them: it is a way of making an indirect connection with the other on one's own terms or on the terms of a
leader who has already done the work of fabricating a meaning.
But it takes great effort to suppress the judgment that the collective is not God, that it is as mutating, unpredictable, and
unforgiving as any individual, and yet lacks its own expressive
center, filling that void with regulations or, at best, the products
of the arts. I do not deny that there are traditions, only that
they are not alive but must be vivified by individuals, and then
it is not the tradition that gains vitality but the individual.
"Humanism" is still a word on many lips and it is even more

deeply rooted in the hearts of those behaviorists and structuralists
who work so hard to abolish the "subject." Humanity is the
target and repository of the modern version of universal love, a
useful fiction for the engineering mind which likes to see its
designs become operational. It is a figment of the nineteenth-
century project of mobilizing disparate loyalties that finds its
personal resonance in the wish that one's life be significant, that
one count for something. But count for whom? Scrutinize closely
enough and everything will have to be for some particular
persons, none of whom has any universal significance and none
of whom can offer anything but relative and vacillating valida-
tion to the meaning-seeker's efforts. The lover of the collective
chases his own tail; he is not the tail of a comet.

I think it safe to say that no society has existed on a foundation of universal love, or of love in general, but only on
particular loves, where service was altogether personal. The
totalitarian experiments of the twentieth century have attempted
to contravene the carnality that is the very basis of society—
and the reference for most of the arts—by regimenting the flesh
and, through it, the substantial self in the service of some transpersonal project. All have failed, even those regimes that retain
the trappings of utopianism. Once the abstractness of the group
becomes obvious to the solitary, all loyalties to collectives or
even to potential appreciating selves are cancelled. All remaining loyalties are to individual selves, who share with one a radical
reality, each uniquely determinate. But even then how restricted must one's love be? A humanitarian impulse built on
compassion might still go out to all contemporary fellow suf-
ferers. And one might, as perhaps Jesus did, make universal love
a matter of loving each individual in one's context of orientation
in (though it is redundant to say so) just the appropriate way.
Free service would then be just that, not only free in the sense
of not being based on need, but also devoid of special affection
and, even for that, not at all aloof or cold. I cannot speak

against this form of universalizing love, because it not only acknowledges but accentuates individuality, so much so that only the momentary experience conditions the loving response. It is the analogue in the realm of love to the Zen life of making each moment perfect. Yet though I can sometimes taste the life of universalizing love I cannot embrace it because its loyalty is ultimately to a loving response to each situation and not to any particular enduring self or selves.

My entire discussion stumbles on particularity, on my inability to take the substantial self out of love, to make the universalizing love that I find in Jesus through St. Francis of Assisi the basis of practicing the virtue of love. The conception of free service is surely a Christian one, though it became evident to me as virtue toward the other when reflecting on the moral writings of the Anglo-Jewish philosopher Samuel Alexander. Free service, of course, came to Alexander by grace of Hegel, who was an unabashedly Christian philosopher. The universalizing of free service seems to be necessitated by the idea of a love that initiates, rather than one that desires. And here we are led to the prime distinction in twentieth-century Swedish evangelical theology, that between *agape* and *eros*. According to the school of Anders Nygren, God's love is completely initiation, and human love never is. *Agape* is nonpossessive love, a pure gift, something that finite personal existents cannot understand but that they can receive. It is a neat solution to the problem of universalizing love to apportion *eros,* the component of love that desires to possess and be possessed, to personal existents; and *agape,* which commits itself gratuitously, though joyfully, to God. Hegel and Nygren lie at opposite poles of the same tradition, the one secularizing *agape* and appearing at times to bureaucratize it, and the other making it entirely supernatural. Neither of them grasps fully that a life of universalizing love is open to anyone who can comprehend what it is, moment by moment. Why would one reject it? Or straightjacket it in social

function? Or put it in God's sole possession? Some particular
individual or individuals must be more important than others,
at least to the self that is dedicated to a graded rather than a
universal love. And this importance cannot be based merely on
having been placed in certain social relations, as the Confucian
proponents of "graded love" taught that it was. The other
selves to whom one's love is directed must be chosen by the
self, indeed, somewhat arbitrarily after the Calvinist fashion. And
then they must call out a loyalty that transcends—though it is
entirely independent of—attraction.

The more securely one installs oneself in one's own life—that is,
the more one becomes habituated to taking the philosophic
standpoint—the more distance one keeps from love. I do not
mean that there is any hatred in philosophy, but that part of the
wisdom it yields is the injunction of the monk Tikhon in Dmitri
Merejkowsky's *Peter and Alexis*: "Love people and flee them."
If one begins philosophizing in the state of a radical separation
suffused with the mood of dread, in which one is constricted by
the finitude of one's momentary experience and through it of
one's life, one will move, if at all, in one of two directions: either
outside one's circle of radical reality and into a state in which
one conceives of oneself as one-among-many, or toward the
center of that circle, the point of pure awareness that opens out
into an englobing consciousness that includes and, therefore,
limits the dread. The sickness unto death has no cure: one either
suffers it full strength, disguises it through the will to believe
(necessary for any of Pascal's "diversions"), or controls it by
containing its overt expressions. Existential philosophy, which
begins with St. Paul's epistles, can never be outmoded because
it responds to the decisive experience of encountering one's em-
bodiment as a finality. Ancient Greek philosophy knew very little
about carnality because it did not incorporate a sense of the
importance of the self for the self, that is, a self-concern, which

is the way that I understand Heidegger's *sorge*. Such self-concern is Jerusalem's legacy to the West, whereas impersonality through the medium of the concept is the West's inheritance from Athens. The existential philosopher strives to combine the particularity of Jerusalem with the generality of the Athenian spirit, a synthesis that can never be achieved, but may nonetheless be attempted, not in a spirit of defiance but in one of joy in putting in public terms what proceeds from one's own intimacy, a discipline that requires expressing other philosophic selves to oneself. The existential philosopher presents reports on what it means to exist as a self-related being (in Kierkegaard's terms, "The self is a relation of itself to itself"). Concretely that means confronting one's being-toward-death and making explicit to oneself what that encounter means. My own move has been to deepen radical separation, to work inward to the point at which I can discriminate over-ego from substantial self and, thereby, observe the sickness unto death as it arises. I do not go outside myself to resolve the problem of my existence, which is another way of saying that love is gratuitous for the philosopher, whose reflections begin in separation and end in solitude.

But must the philosopher flee people? Love's gratuity distances it from philosophy; enacted love subverts philosophy. Yet love is the crowning virtue that philosophy must acknowledge and thereby surrender its own pretensions to judge. The cultivation of the philosophic standpoint means a fleeing from people, if not in space by becoming more or less a hermit, then by silently placing oneself above the others, rooting them within one's own radical reality. Love undercuts that personal seat of judgment, making the self immediately relative to another radical reality, to a personal existent to whom the self accords, in Josiah Royce's terms, acknowledgment. In the case of love it is a full acknowledgment, in the sense that the other self is not merely felt to relativize one's self but becomes a recipient of one's devotion. Love scandalizes all philosophy by its particu-

larity and existential philosophy specifically by its requirement
that one surrender—though surely not altogether?—one's
autonomous judgment. Existential philosophy could limp along
on Sartre's account of the other as a drain into which my world
is sucked; he described a minimal acknowledgment demanded
by a war, the object of which for each one is to remain apart
from (not be incorporated by) the others. But love acknowledges maximally, by making the other's centricity an imperative
reference of one's own concerns. Suddenly the context of
orientation does not belong to the self alone, but is a medium
between selves. This does not mean an adherence to Ortega's
reformulation of his earlier "my life is the radical reality," into
"our life is the radical reality." There is no one to possess a
common life. Nor does it mean adopting the interpretation of
oneself as one among many others, as the member of some society or community, which, for a reflective self aware of its
singularity, can only be a circumstantial determination, not a
self-definition. Love does not lead to self-objectification, as do
social ideas based on group membership, but to the encounter of
subject with subject, of one center of personal existence with
another. The other center is as absolute as oneself and if it does
not know itself to be such, then the lover must strive to create
that awareness. The ultimate aim of love is to free, not to
possess, the other. Eros, love as desire, is an interlude in tracts
of time devoted to love as service: it is the other as other who is
loved virtuously, not the other as an extension of oneself. This
helps illuminate a point made earlier that one cannot in a full
sense love an object, including an ideal. An object can only
be appreciated in its relation to the self, in the way that it is for
the self, whereas the other self, for the lover, is appreciated for
itself. If one values an object for what it can do for others,
that, of course, is love for the others, not for the object.

What a cold and stark view of love I seem to be presenting,
one that seems to take all the joy out of it. I am aware of all the

pleasures love brings and also of its sorrows, but I must remind
that I have been concerned with describing how love appears
in the good life as one of its virtues. As a virtue love must be as
much from the self, that is, from the solitary self, as are self-
control and artistry. I have been speaking of the kind of love
that a radically individuated self can express, not that which
such a self might have experienced on the way to individuation.
Most of what is called love has a great admixture of need and
of a consequent sense of dependence. Is it wise to remove these
elements from love and defend a love so free that it is in danger
of becoming superfluous, if not for the loved one then for the
lover? I would prefer to think of the love I am describing
here not as superfluous but as fearless, and by that I do not mean
courageous and heroic, but simply as not being motivated by fear
of the loss of the loved one. Love as a virtue frees service
from dependence on the other; it is no longer conditional upon
being served or even upon gaining approval. I am less certain
that love can or should be independent of spontaneous attraction, of an erotic element, that, at a minimum, is delighted with
the delight of others and at a maximum relishes being loved,
that is, being served. An important aspect of loving is receiving
the love of others wholeheartedly, giving way to it at times so
that communion is achieved. But the initiation, the giving to the
other, is prior when love is considered a virtue to the receiving
and, thus, to the reciprocity of giving and receiving. And even
when the lover's radical reality has been disrupted and deranged
by the other's upsurge—an "uprooting" to follow Ortega's
terminology—the exercise of love proceeds from a reconsti-
tuted radical reality, that is, the other must be continually re-
rooted in one's life and one's free judgment reestablished, just for
one to be able to love. The scandal of love creates inescapable
contradictions for philosophy.

The loved one destroys the lover's centricity by revealing that
there exists another radical reality beside the lover's own. And

it is rooted in that reality that the lover must serve. Love, which
is so much absorbed in art, which takes artistry beyond itself,
is also surrender. When one loves one is on the lover's turf, a
radical reality rooted in another radical reality, surely a contradiction in terms, but also real enough, because it is possible to
experience this kind of virtuous love. But it is also true that
one, or at least I, cannot love this way very often or for very
long. And, as I have remarked, I should not because I cannot
serve freely but from my own radical reality. Love and freedom:
there is love's agony, in the sense of the great Hispanic
pensadores such as Unamuno and Vaz Ferreira. Tragedy, for
the agonic *pensador,* is being unable to have all the good at
once. It is rooted, of course, in the deeper despair over nothingness, but so long as one is astride Rosinante, affirming life,
that despair has been inspirited by vivacity. And Sancho must
also have his say: pull back into your circle. Freedom and love.
Love for freedom. Freedom for love. The *pensador* has very
little patience for the discrimination of knower from field, for
the ultimate freedom of standing above life. He would spend
everything on love, tossing away self-control and artistry, to
consume himself faster, but then he pulls himself back into his
absolute personality. And so there is a moment of patience, of
extreme discrimination of knower from field in the *pensador's*
repertory of experience. Unamuno was a great philologist and
even a greater author of fictions or metafictions. Spanish irony
creates a withering distance, daring the other self not to take one
seriously; there is no surrender here. Is this kind of *macho*
spirit the kind of individuality required for exercising the virtue
of free service? Proud love. Can there be such a thing? The
Spanish mystics know of nothing else. Can I have myself and
be devoted to the other? But I must have myself if I am to be
devoted to the other. And I cannot have both simultaneously.
To conform myself to the other is not merely to alter my moods
and desires, but to enter into another field, to decenter myself,
to extrospect. Such extrospection is as genuine an orientation as is

projecting oneself into the future (prospection) or remembering (retrospection). It is adaptation to the other as a free judge
of existence. And it is such a free judge whom I must love.

Love, this sort of recognition of the other that passes into
service, cannot tolerate any but a derived or founded "we."
What a terrible surrender Ortega made when he declared at the
end of his career that "our life is the radical reality." "We are"
only in the abstract sense in which we are able to think or consider ourselves to be one-among-many. "We" is a convention
founded on identification. Its best use is to point to various
collections of personal existents who partake in mutually sustaining relations. The reality of the collection inheres in the
common objects that orient the various personal existents toward
one another, in the satisfaction that those objects provide for
desires, and in any love that unites free persons. The "we,"
however, can be cancelled by any self that possesses its own life
simply by failing to use it as an orienting idea, which is all that
it is. It is a serious mistake, then, to believe that love for another
should lead to the dissolution of both selves into some sort
of common life. The substantial selves of two free individuals
may be so consonant, so attuned to one another, that they often
judge in what seems to be—and there is no reason in this case
to believe that appearance is deceptive—exactly the same
fashion. And this unison is almost always strengthened by a
stable field of common objects. Why not say that such unison
constitutes a genuine "we?" I cannot object to such a usage in
principle, because I believe that communion is a necessary condition for being able to acknowledge another self as self,
though not fully as other self. And there is the problem when we
are speaking of free individuals that they must assert their freedom even as they surrender themselves in love. Love, for free
individuals, does not abolish the otherness of the other but bends
before it unbending. Communion not only provides one of the
requisites for love, but it is also a fruition of love, whose

instances are more frequent the more service is mutual and, therefore, the more lovers become familiar with one another's worlds. Yet however closely bound substantial selves may become to one another they are relative to different bodies and different centers of awareness, and the whole individual may reject communion, not only out of self-assertive rebellion, but also out of love, out of concern for the other's freedom. It is because love is dedicated to freedom, that is, to freeing the loved one through service, that it cannot tolerate any but a derived "we." Eros craves communion and in its pursuit of it contrives a "we." Virtuous love restrains Eros, placing devotion beyond the desire to possess and be possessed. But it must also be turned back to enhance Eros, another of love's ironies, if not one of its contradictions.

 Love is an initiated surrender that keeps the initiative. If that seems too brutal, one should remember that the service involved in love is to a great part taken up with helping to satisfy desires, the fulfillment of many of which involves pleasure for the giver as well as the receiver. The desire for communion is widespread, deep, and genuine, and to cultivate and enjoy its satisfaction is delightful. It is also delightful—that is the best English term I know of, with all of its connotations of buoyancy, to describe the pleasures attending love—merely to witness the other achieve freedom and gain the sense of power that, for Nietzsche, throbbed at the center of an ascending life. And there is the compassion that sustains ministering to declining life, loving even the decaying and diseased flesh, not in spite of its weakness but because it is the flesh of a person. I cannot call that compassion a pleasure, but it is a great good, something worthwhile that comes from a troubled acceptance—not an embrace—of the destructive aspects of nature. The various boons of love, which many people receive even when they have not fully and reflectively grasped love as free service, may all be gathered under the disposition of cherishing the other. Loving service is free, but it cherishes, even though that cherishing does not cancel love's agony; the other must, again, be irretrievably other for love to be virtuous. To cherish means to possess the other in such a way that the other's independence is not violated, that the other's life is strengthened, which is another contradiction in terms, but one which stands for an experience that can be enjoyed. Cherishing involves standing above the other, letting the other be defined by one's own estimation of what is precious, yet finding what is precious in the other's spontaneous self-expressions or revelations of self. But love cannot be exhausted by cherishing, because the feeling that the other is precious comes and goes with the vicissitudes of the substantial self; and love—which is not, as discussed here, universal, but for a particular self—must abide, just as self-control must.

One only enters into the other's field, becomes rooted in the other's radical reality (though of course never actually so), by being taken into it. One cannot fully serve another self unless one has been drawn into its circle so that one can understand what appropriate service means. Before one can love another in the virtuous sense, one must be trusted by the other; one is drawn in by being entrusted with the other's primary expressions of life and attending to their meaning, not as they relate to one's own interests but to those of the other; that is, one must attempt to take up the other's standpoint in the world, to represent the other to oneself, finally, to identify with the other. The more the other has succeeded in coordinating the complexity of the substantial self without repressing it or masking it by reaction formation, the more arduous, but also the more gratifying, will be the discipline of appreciating the other self. Narrow and rigidified selves can only be served in the most external sense of satisfying their organic desires and some of their rudimentary emotional yearnings. Delusional selves cannot be served at all, because they demand completely bound service, which would cancel the self of the servant, or they refuse service altogether, an extreme case of the latter being catatonic schizophrenia and another autism. Delusion means that the other as other is not given a welcome, but is rejected or interpreted according to one of the projections of the delusional self: the other is not trusted. Rigid selves extend a restricted welcome and tend toward rejection or projection, falling short of them only by continual recurrence to the rebellious "me" which sets up a defense of impenetrable particularity. The generous self is capable of being loved more fully than the intolerant one, because it loves: love begets love and is reciprocal when it reaches its perfection. But love does not aim at that perfection: one must be loved in order to love, but one does not love in order to be loved. Being entrusted with the other is the first moment in the dialectic of love, one that precedes or is coordinate with initiation.

I speak here, of course, of love at its highest peak, which in-volves selves in charge of their own lives, so self-controlled that they wish to incorporate even more diversity into the substantial ego. Such selves, in which over-ego and substantial self are highly discriminated, readily extend welcomes but become im-patient at rigidity and unbending to delusion—though they may feel compassion for those who suffer both and serve them to the degree that they can be served freely. The lover strives to en-hance the freedom of the other and tires with failure. Or, better, the lover does not so much tire as become perfunctory, because as an initiative love is, in great part, independent of its proximate effects: the lover knows that sometimes one will be rejected and, contradictory as it may seem, continue to serve. But service in the face of hatred, though it is necessarily a part of love, will eventually lead to the destruction of love's initiative, just because it bespeaks a futile resistance to the desire of the other to expel the self from its field. Just when love is most needed, when the loved one is most consumed by the hatred of existence, love will nearly always fail. No service is then possible and in its place may grow a resentment against the other for being unworthy of one's love, which is the very negation or antithesis of love. Love is an initiative within a context of its acceptance. The loved one must accept the lover, at least to the extent of welcoming the service, if not always the servant. Kant's ethic is admirable for stressing the initiative of the self, but it leaves out, as the condition for the significance of that initiative, the trust of the other for the self. It does not matter whether or not one tells the truth or keeps a promise if the other self does not care or throws it back in one's face. For Kant, of course, the categorical imperative was to be willed because of its rational appeal, with no conditions on its exercise: the only good without limitation is a good will. But a good will only operates concretely when it is accepted; there can be no good will toward another self who rejects one's service. Or is the most demanding of services to serve against rejection? And to serve in that most peripheral way, which may turn out to be the most central, of holding oneself in readiness to serve? Kant knew nothing of such paradoxes of the good will. For purposes of philosophy he did not care about the operation of the will, believing that to do so would involve him in measuring goodness by its consequences. He overlooked the condition for the intelligibility of the good will, a self who is open to receive the service it actuates. Is the first duty to receive? Thou shalt take the other seriously as a truth-teller, as a promise keeper, as someone who is dependable, even though one knows that nobody is to be trusted because the substantial self is so variable. Or, better, trust in a narrow and rigid self is cheap, whereas trust in a highly differentiated self is dear, unwarranted (even if it is never betrayed), and essential to the perfection of love as an initiating activity, a virtue. Yet as love reaches its fruition it transcends both the other's trust and one's trust in the other, and expends itself for the other. And it may sometimes become so independent of trust that it enters into the other's field secretly so that the other never knows the author of what seems to befall it as good fortune.

When one trusts and is trusted by the other the initiative of love is supported by a process of mutual appreciation that allows each one to know the other. In the absence of appreciation of the other there is possibility for only the more external forms of service, the ones directed to catering to interests widely shared, either by the members of the human species as such or by those who belong to some more particular group. The most excellent service is performed by one who is well versed in the shifting moods of the other self and, most important in the multifarious gratifications and dissatisfactions that the other feels. Such knowledge is not available unless the other reveals it, which occurs when the other is trusting or desperate. In the latter case the other feels a deep need to be served, to be the only center of free expression, all the while demanding that the servant be wiser and more capable than itself and, therefore, above it and, indeed, englobing it. The desperate other wants the self's devotion without the self; it wants an effaced self that is never on its own time, even when it has been temporarily rejected. It wants service to be free and yet totally bound and that in principle, not as a result of some fortuitous conditions. All selves who have known what it is to be loved may be prone to ask for such miracles. One wishes for a genie who not only performs but deeply sympathizes. The trusting self is at the antipodes from the desperate self, and seeks to elicit the other's varied expressions of life so that it can draw the other into its field, the better to serve it. Mutual love is marvelous because it orients each one toward the other, gaining the service of the other by serving the other through trusting and being trusted. One gains the service of the other by drawing the other into one's ambit, by a welcome of the other as other, thereby making the other free through that welcome. Trust for the trusting self becomes a phase of initiating love itself, which is another paradox of love, not a contradiction that annuls it, as does that of the desperate self.

Love, as are all of the virtues, is a finite possibility within a finite life. Even after it makes its first appearance in a personal existence it is never entirely constant, alternating necessarily with frequent moments of self-assertion and self-possession. And that is not even to speak of the wayward substantial self which is spontaneously attracted to all sorts of other selves that display some similarity to those that called out its primary identifications and cathexes, thereby leading to conflicts of loyalty. There is no escape from the conclusion that love demands loyalty and that loyalty requires fidelity in the face of temptation. There is no cheap loyalty for a self that does not close itself off from the full range of its interests. Indeed, the more one appreciates others, the more one will be impelled to love them, to take an initiative in their lives. Such an initiative is undertaken for the other self as an existent with temporal extension, not merely for that self in one of its momentary experiences: love "binds time," to use Robert MacIver's admirable phrase. Too many initiatives in too many other lives build up obligations that are bound to come into conflict. There is an exclusivity involved in love for a particular self, which means that universal love would have to be universally practiced if it were to replace particular loves. The generality of human beings accepts, indeed welcomes, the fact that love is graded, that each is not equally important to each, and endorses particular loyalties. This is the closest most people get to affirming Josiah Royce's "loyalty to loyalty," which in actual life is far from being an overriding principle, but ordinarily functions to affirm each one's own right to a particular love or, at best, to foster a respect for an opponent, even as warfare is pursued. Though love is inconstant it is still possible to speak of a life of love in which one is oriented continually to recuperating one's love for another self.

It is this orientation or commitment that is the essence of the concrete loyalty to another self and not actual constancy of service, which would annul itself into servitude. There is, however, a demand deeply rooted within many, if not all, personal existents for just the sort of constancy of service that is impossible to achieve, particularly on a basis of free service. Indeed, any demand for another's service or even an expectation of it is subversive of love, though it need not destroy it in a particular case in which the initiating aspect of love has been heightened. The desperate lover may be understood from another viewpoint as one who has remained a child. Nobody, it seems, grows up entirely, in the sense of losing (rather than suppressing) the wish to be delivered into the care of another. If the generality of people recognizes the supremacy of graded love over universal love, it is unprepared to accept the condition that love is not a substitute for care for oneself but is an opportunity to give and, when love has been perfected, to receive a free gift. As Paul of Tarsus recognized, the most pervasive obstacle to love is not brute hatred but the sense of justice and appeal to the law. Freud understood that the sense of justice grows up in the playroom, when the child who no longer harbors the implicit expectation of being cared for unreservedly bids for the next best thing, which is at least as much as the others have. The claim to be treated justly involves making the self other to itself, evacuating from it the specificity and uniqueness of its own desires and substituting for them supposedly general and common interests, which for some reason or just on their face, ought to be honored. I am not here smirking at or denigrating justice, but only deriving it from the failure of the more primal demand for total care to be satisfied. Appeals to justice are suffused with resentment, that is, they are instances of what Nietzsche called *ressentiment,* which may be understood as a compromise formation between the wish to be served steadfastly and spontaneously, and recognition of the fact that if one

is going to be served at all one must either sacrifice in some
way for that service or be loved, which latter, if it is to achieve
fullness, must be accompanied by one's own love for the servant.
Love demands a firm sense of one's own limitation by the other
and of the other as the finite and free recipient of one's care.
Love reaches a fruition when each is devoted to the other, but is
gratified and, therefore, grateful, and not expectant and demanding, when the other shows devotion. Justice, in contrast, is
jealous, ever on the defensive, because it stems from the attempt
to elude the adverse aspects of existence. The wish for a genie
arises, I believe, from the same condition to which Dewey traced
the quest for certainty; the radical vulnerability of the personal
existent, the risk inherent in life, that is, human subjection to
death, disease, and decay. One longs for the ideal mother or
father and such yearnings are readily transferred to an idea of
God, to a leader, and/or, most often, to another personal existent
with whom one is in direct interchange. But the substitute
protector and nurturer always fails and then Job's complaint is
sounded: I deserve better than I have gotten. As Unamuno
noted, each of us deserves everything good, insofar as we want
it. Indeed, we deserve what we want, because rights are merely
socially expedient ways of couching our desires. But that has
nothing to do with love, which is a virtue that depends upon
sufficient self-control to temper the "me."

It is only because love is inconstant that one of its aspects is
loyalty, the commitment to recuperate love in the face of one's
failure to love. Loyalty may be considered an extension of trust,
both an effort to make oneself trustworthy once one has called
out trust in the other, and a determination to renew one's trust
in the other when the other seems to have betrayed it. Love
is ceaselessly shadowed by the primal betrayals that first set the
self into a rebellious posture: it must be exercised against
the evidence that the other is undependable and is sometimes
indifferent or malign, as well as against one's betrayals of the

other. Loyalty, as it is used here, is similar to Gabriel Marcel's
"secondary reflection," which is reconsidering what one has done
in a situation from all points of view concerned, not only one's
own. Loyalty lives on "secondary reflection," deepening it to a
resolve to appreciate the other, even when the other has been
malign and has evoked one's own self-righteousness, and most
important, when one has acted out of hatred or lack of concern
for the other and is susceptible to projecting that maleficence
onto the other. But how can service be free if it depends upon
such binding of time? Again freedom and love collide. It is
no solution to maintain that one freely commits oneself to the
other in a certain moment and then is bound by that commitment: the free judge holds all commitments to be revocable and
acknowledges all projects to be finite. Loyalty becomes martyrdom or sacrifice to another finite self when the other has too
intense and manifest a hatred of existence. And, though an
infinite and saving God may make martyrdom seem sublime, a
finite self never can do so, which, of course, does not mean that
the free servant's loyalty may not issue in the sacrifice of self,
of one's own radical reality, for the other—which, indeed, in
some small part it always does. Another paradox of love.

Within the context of loyal love the other moments of the
dialectic of love unfold. Trust, which allows for the appreciation of the other's particularity by giving the other opportunities
and encouragement for expression of a wide range of responses
to life, ripens into a more active and intrusive acceptance of the
other, which was best described by Gabriel Marcel in his discussion of *disponibilité* (availability). Availability, which may
be conceived of alternately as the second moment of the
dialectic of love or as an extension and deepening of its first
moment, trust, is analogous to the phase of self-control that was
denominated inner tolerance. To be available to the other is to
be attentive to and tolerant of the variations in the other's

substantial self, to be receptive to the other's moods and to discern the other's interests. There is a readiness to serve and an alertness to the opportunities for appropriate service that make availability distinguishable from trust: the available self has decentered itself by entering into the other's field as a reality on the way to being rooted in it but that then pulls back and holds itself ready to judge how to initiate its service for the other. Availability shows better than any of the other aspects of love the tension between freedom and deliverance that is always present and never fully resolved in a loving orientation. The available self is delivered to the other in the sense of being occupied with the signs, which are often unconscious, that the other is giving or has given of desires and fears; but is receptive to these signs only for the purpose of serving the other's good, that is, drawing the other toward a more virtuous life, freeing the other. Availability, therefore, is not neutral, but is for the other's virtue, not for the mere gratification of the other's desires. This does not mean, however, that the available self has plans for the other or wishes to transform the other into a particular kind of substantial self. The lover's aim is the freedom of the loved one, and this freedom is not enhanced by modeling the other, but by all of the measures that increase the other's feeling of power, especially those that provide the other with the confidence to undertake disciplines of self-control and to master the practice of the arts. Availability is oriented toward permitting the specific virtues of the other to become manifest. Their manifestation, however, will be the result of the other's own initiative and not of the available self's agency. The available self must be for the other's better self, not as the available self might imagine it to be, but as it is continually revealed in new ways by the other.

The structure of availability shows a major difference between artistry and love. For the artist the material—though it is independent of the mental design that it is to display, and

though it restricts the range of designs appropriate to it—is
taken up into the artist's design and, within the limits of the art
in question, exhausted by it. Art does not free material but
subjects it through the various kinds of artistry, though some of
the objects of some of the arts can be appreciated for themselves with no reference beyond the responses of the appreciator.
The lover, in contrast, is disposed to free the other, which means
that the artistic phase of love—the lover's positive interventions
to alter the loved one's field—must be subordinate to the
loved one's freedom to reject initiatives in favor of other de-
terminations, although as is always the case with love, this
principle may be overridden by the lover when it is deemed
necessary to force the loved one to be free. Love works between
the lover's and the loved one's judgments, sometimes approaching a creative act and sometimes approaching a form of servitude. It flourishes most at a midpoint between the two extremes,
at which the loving self holds its own judgments and those of
the loved one in a reciprocal relation, allowing each side to
inform the other, thereby permitting mutual criticism of intentions based on hatred or indifference. In art, of course, there is
no such reciprocal criticism, but only a monitoring of how successfully the material is being brought into conformity with the
design, even if that design emerges within a creative process
over a chain of moments. As in the art of politics, the design may
be of human behavior itself, which implies relations among
selves but prescinds from their spontaneity. However, one might
project one fulfillment of the political art as a state of civic
friendship, in Jacques Maritain's terms, which is here understood
as a cultivated disposition to cherish, though in relatively limited
ways, the others with whom one comes in contact and even
those with whom one has only mediate relations (perhaps one
passes over the boundary of love here or at least reaches it).
Art also does not display the bivalent character of service,
which is disclosed in availability as a readiness not only to inter-

vene in the other's field but also to be served by the other. One of love's paradoxes is that often the greatest encouragement to virtue is to be served, to give oneself over to the care of the other. One serves here by being served. The fruit of persistent cultivation of availability is a wisdom to know when it is appropriate to stand for the other, to take the other's place in satisfying an interest, and when to let the other take over an aspect of one's own life. It may even be necessary to be available by appearing to be out of reach, as when the other needs to gain self-possession in solitude or can be served best by other selves. Being out of reach is at the margins (or beyond them) of availability, as is its polar opposite, communion, when, to use scholastic terminology, the potency of readiness is transformed into the act of mutual enjoyment.

As a moment of loyal love availability must transcend any gratifications the self receives from the other, although it surely need not eschew them and, indeed, thrives upon them. Such satisfactions given by the other include not only objects and activities that fulfill specific desires of the self, but also delight in the other's freedom—their unique enactment of virtue—and joy in the other's love. The special happiness that comes from loving and being loved, the at-homeness with the other that eventuates in frequent moments of a rich communion involving a broad range of each substantial self, fortifies loyalty and results in more appropriate initiatives of the lover in the loved one's field. Love as a virtue seizes upon such delight and joy to enhance the lover's own spirit of good heartedness, what the Confucian philosophers call "jen" and Matthew Arnold termed "sweetness and light." Service cannot be loving if it is not given with a committed freedom that evinces happiness in giving and grateful affirmation of the other. Yet such full-blooded cherishing is only a sporadic occurrence, because the substantial self is so variable, and it must often be supplemented by forms of service that appear to defeat their purpose by withdrawing affection at the very moment of providing concrete aid. The available self makes its fullest contribution to love when its welcome to the other is unequivocal, even if silent. But in any given case a wholehearted welcome may be succeeded by an assertion of the "me," which undoes the initial good and must be compensated for by action sustained by one's allegiance to the other and not by joy in service. The recourse to hard-bitten service is minimized most effectively by cultivating the two virtues that support love: self-control and artistry. The discrimination of over-ego from substantial self, the heightening of which is the fruit of self-control, is attended by a benignity that permits good heartedness and a sweet and enlightened temperament to take hold unreservedly. The perfection of artistry, particularly in the practice of the fundamental arts, builds a sense of power that allows the lover to serve without being frustrated by the failures and exertions that occur in the absence of skill. The virtue of love is the most difficult of all to practice, because its proper exercise depends upon cultivating the other main virtues and, more important, because it is so difficult to become attuned to the other self. Availability is so central to love because it is the practice of such attunement. It is here that love most frequently fails, and the more one is aware of this moment of love, the more one realizes that love usually misses its mark.

Beyond attunement, which is achieved in the moment of availability, is the more active intervention into the other's field in which one attempts to alter its content, what Heidegger called leaping-in for the other. Though it seems paradoxical, it is just at those moments in which attunement is least likely to be achieved—that is, when self and other are in conflict or when either one or both has succumbed to fear—that it is most likely that the self will leap in to alter the other's field as an act of transcending love. This novel eruption breaks a previous consensus and imposes a new norm by its performance, risking the other's rejection or loss, or overcoming the self's own hatred or fear to force its goodness upon the other, its love of life. Not everything can be decided by conversation, Jurgen Habermas notwithstanding. Evil has such firm root in our lives that we torture one another with projections of our own failures, from the torture chambers of political police to the private hells we create for one another with insincere love. And love must often be insincere to remain love through an outbreak of hatred for existence. And one is in hell if the other demands affection that is not there because one is grappling with the sickness unto death. Among selves that have achieved a familiarity with self-control and sufficient artistry to care for themselves as solitary beings, hatred of existence is an ever-present shadow that the darkest cell cannot obliterate; it is yet darker. In the service of life itself, that self rebels against the lover just so it will have the solitude to fall back upon its radical separation and gather strength for a new assault toward virtue. It is here that leaping-in is perfected. The self seizes the opportunity and in some way acts so as to make the other decide in a more profound way about their being, risking failure by deliberately deciding on something new that will alter the prominence or importance of elements in the other's field. However subtle and devoid of physical coercion the intervention may be (how does Habermas deal with someone who refuses to join the dialogue?), such leaping-in is violent. This is the perfection—free risk by the self of itself and the other, of the possibility of their entry into one another's fields—of the more general form of intervening to alter the other's field to make some improvement in it. But the violence of choosing for the other, which is most prominent in intimate relations among free selves, is present even in the most indirect or mediate relations, such as the production of standardized goods to serve international markets.

By imposing something on the other, leaping-in closes the openness of the self to the other that is the essence of *disponibilité.* Any "doing-for" makes an alternative impossible, binds time through an action. And simply to coexist with each other as selves, we must act, force ourselves on the other, make ourselves obtrusive as selves. At the margins we effect meaningful change upon each other through the practice of the arts and at the core through what Unamuno called impressing ourselves upon others. Making such an impression, calling out from the other identification or cathexis may be regarded as the essence of what Heidegger called leaping-ahead, holding out an example for others. Heidegger's discussion focuses one's attention on the prominence of leaping-ahead in the educational relation: the teacher does not merely "do for" the student in the sense of giving the student a mental supplement, providing information and certification, but more important, from the viewpoint of virtuous teaching, by evincing a standard of performance that the student may be inspired to emulate. I am here assimilating leaping-ahead to leaping-in; the former is a way of doing the latter, though one which is apparently more distant than being a stand-in, a supplement. If one thinks, however, of powerful personalities and their influence, the decisive element in leaping-ahead becomes prominent. Unamuno understood the preceding point and offered the brilliant interpretation of love as "mutual imposition" and "invasive charity." He counseled in *The Tragic Sense of Life* that one discharge the duties of one's station in the spirit of the shoemaker who would create such wonderful shoes that he would be deemed irreplaceable by his patrons. And on a level of intimacy what does the lover do but attempt to set an example for giving and receiving concernful pleasure, becoming thereby irreplaceable? Here, indeed, is a union of leaping-ahead and the more supplementary form of leaping-in, "invasive charity" in a full-blooded sense. And here, as Unamuno understood, is where the limits of the more active intervention into the other's field are reached and often breached, negating love itself. Service may make the other a dependent, begin to cater to the other's cravings to decline initiative, and then rouse impulses to domination in the giver. At its perfection leaping-in takes over the other's life for but a moment, fulfilling the other's freedom by determining a choice, reducing a range of possibilities to "yes" or "no." But that perfection must be momentary and pursued rarely with fear and trembling. One is responsible for one's own love, just as the doctor is finally responsible for the patient, but the lover must be as an ideal doctor, who would attend as fully and intently as possible to the patient's expressions of and judgments on the disease and on the effects of the therapies employed to treat it. Loving service, even in the intensive-care unit where leaping-in is starkly revealed as an active initiative to alter the other's field, is meant to free the other.

All virtue arises from the initiative of the free self, and it is this that guides the lover's free initiatives to free the other self. The final moment of the dialectic of love is renouncing initiative and leaving the other absolutely free to determine him- or herself, letting the other be, allowing the other to take risks, experiment with abandon, be liberated from the bonds of the prior moments of love. Even the bonds of the self's loyalty to the other, which loyalty always includes the option (or is it the necessity?) of leaping-in to perpetuate the love and, thereby, to save the other for life? Love and freedom. Freedom and love. The two are only reconciled when freedom is for love and love is for freedom. And love misses the mark so often and is lost to hatred even more frequently. The virtuous self is directed to perfection and generous to failure. In such a posture life in the light of finitude seems to be worthy of the affirmation from which it arises.

I should not leave you in the world of virtue that I have constructed for myself. For myself. And, of course, I also have offered it to you in as philosophical a form as I possibly could. I would not expect anyone to adopt the ideas contained in the preceding essay as guides to his or her own life, but if I have succeeded in my purpose those spirits who are congenial to mine, who live their circumstances in a fashion similar to the way I do, will find reasoned corroboration for their assents and, perhaps, a bit of a push forward in their struggles, which must be their own and finally be expressed in their own words. If any less congenial spirits have travelled this far with me I hope without expectation that they have acquired a sharper sense of the plurality of mentalities that rise up to confront a troubling world. I began to philosophize when I read George Santayana's *Dominations and Powers* nearly twenty years ago. Though since then I have added to his vitalism of the "primal will" and his ironical contemplation of it—an existential note that became prominent when the beast obtruded itself—I still take philosophy as he did, as a personal discipline with a possibly general import. It is an offering not to the gods, as Heidegger might have wished, but to individuals of flesh and bone who must fight to get above themselves to review their very particularized lives and perspectives on their environs. Philosophy's most intimate function, which is the basis of its civilizing role of providing provisional unities to diverse human pursuits, is to show by example how a reflective review of life, as experienced from within, may be attempted. In this sense, philosophies are always by and for individuals, for those who make them and for those who appropriate them for their own living or to heighten the sense of their own relativity to others, to the Other.

I want to stress the social aspect of philosophy, its being a personal art fulfilled in its status as an offering. Not a gift, because that would be making far more of it than it deserves. Philosophy is such a problematic effort that to ask that it be taken seriously bespeaks misplaced pride, which is far different than the native arrogance it accentuates, the arrogance of trying to think things through for oneself. The history of philosophy is a treasure trove of offerings and if one ventures the risk and then finds satisfaction in some of them, there will, happily, always be many more, at least enough for a finite life. And one need not keep to the highways of great tradition; the back roads are filled with the disciplined imaginations, now memories to be revived, of those who undertook what the Mexican philosopher José Vasconcelos called "a sincere examination of the heart," which led him to the kind of "happy pessimism" (*pesimismo alegre*) I have here called "vivacious despair." I need but briefly say that the thoughts that make up my essay were not mere concoctions of an untutored imagination. The pages have been dotted with allusions primarily to those who have influenced me most, whom I have welcomed as kindred spirits with something to teach me—that is, the naturalists and vitalists, and the existentialists. Miguel de Unamuno, Henri Bergson, George Santayana, William James, Alfred North Whitehead, John Dewey, and Samuel Alexander have all helped me grasp the sense of concrete life and to acknowledge levels of intention not coherently expressed in reflective thought. And, perhaps, along these lines I have learned the most from Friedrich Nietzsche and Sigmund Freud, and those, such as Georg Groddeck, Wilhelm Stekel, Carl Jung, and Alfred Adler, who followed Freud's lead. José Ortega y Gasset, Jean-Paul Sartre, Martin Heidegger, Albert Camus, Max Stirner, Irving Babbitt, and John Henry Newman aided me, in contrast, to grasp my own life as glimpsed from a conscious center of expressive imagination through reflective thought. The counterpoint between what Santayana called the "psyche," that partially submerged dynamism of life with its multiple and uncontrollable directions, and the "spirit," that detached and accepting gaze, is an inner dialectic that has structured all of my philosophical thinking. Here it is expressed as the contraposition of momentary experience (the vital present) and personal existence (the radical reality of my temporalized life). If the philosophy I have exposed is inserted into the modern tradition (a paradox itself unless one is glib enough to pronounce modernity at an end), it should be called "critical vitalism." The vitalism is the substantive, because it is life on which I base all else, and even further, on momentary experience of life to begin with. But I am not a classical vitalist who believes in a life principle that outruns my own flesh. I take life as grasped from within by a center that knows itself to be finite and dependent, and yet, absolute; hence, the modifier "critical," which incorporates the existential component.

Where does a "critical vitalism," an ontology that has yielded "finite perfection" as its axiological expression, fit into contemporary philosophical discourse? Its primary public function, I think, should be to serve as a corrective to all those contemporary modes of thought that prescind from the intimacy of subjectivity in order, as Quebec philosopher Fernand Dumont puts it, to construct systems of "operations" that can be manipulated externally. Behaviorism, structuralism, and linguistic analysis are reflections of and contributors to the externalization of the mind. And they find ready contexts of orientation in the collective doctrines of liberal corporatism and Marxism that dominate public discourse today. As correctives, critical vitalism and the pursuit of finite perfection are ways to reclaim the mind for the unique and intimate center of imaginative expression. They indicate that personality is not something to be taken for granted, that merely grows, but is something that can be lost and that, therefore, must be protected and cultivated. They are vindications of finite life, and as such they find congenial company with the various current efforts to revive the generous insights of early twentieth-century philosophy: the return to American classical philosophy, the rehabilitation of Nietzsche, the stormy reinterpretations of Freud, the concerns with historical interpretation, the multifarious phenomenological investigations, and the ferment in Catholic theology. In each of these tendencies there is a return to personal existence, with due regard (perhaps too much regard) for circumstantiality. A radical claim would be that critical vitalism would give to these kindred currents a focus, even a *raison d'être,* the defense of ourselves against ourselves. Again a hope without expectation, but a necessary hope for the native arrogance of a philosopher to project: it is essential to a discourse that is acutely conscious of its relativity and still totalizes, though provisionally. Can the vivacity of finite perfection provide some compensation for the despair of personal existence? We have our lives here and now to win.

Name Index

Acton, T., 101
Adler, A., 67, 163
Alexander, S., 1, 7–8, 10, 12, 19, 21–22, 31, 41, 42, 45, 89, 105, 109, 138, 162
Aristotle, 4, 122
Arnold, M., 54, 156
Augustine, 5

Babbitt, I., 3, 7, 83, 163
Bateman, J., 47
Beethoven, L., 126
Bentley, A., 118
Bergson, H., 9, 10, 162
Buber, M., 122

Camus, A., 11, 128, 163
Canetti, E., 70
Caso, A., 10
Coleridge, S., 124

Descartes, R., 17
Dewey, J., 7, 10, 13, 29, 30, 33, 64, 89, 90, 96, 99, 104, 105, 118, 125, 126, 128, 152, 162
Dostoevsky, F., 76, 125, 127
Dumont, F., 163

Eckhardt, 67
Eichmann, A., 94
Epicurus, 80

Forster, E. M., 128
Francis of Assissi, 138
Freud, S., 2, 59, 61, 64, 65, 67, 68, 69, 70, 76, 77, 93, 103, 151, 163, 164

Groddeck, G., 163

Habermas, J., 158
Hegel, G. W. F., 138
Heidegger, M., 23, 29, 50, 56, 68, 122, 128, 140, 157, 159, 161, 163
Herrigel, E., 116, 119

Hobbes, T., 100, 101
Hocking, W. E., 101
Hughes, H., 96

James, W., 2, 4, 7, 32, 39, 51, 61, 82, 83, 162
Jesus, 137, 138
Jung, C. G., 38, 69, 163

Kant, I., 148
Kierkegaard, S., 65, 128, 140
Kroker, A., 82

Locke, J., 12

Machiavelli, N., 5, 100, 102
MacIntyre, A., 4–5
MacIver, R., 150
Marcel, G., 22, 153
Maritain, J., 155
Merejkowsky, D., 139
Mill, J. S., 101

Newman, J. H., 17, 27, 163
Nicholas of Cusa, 19
Nietzsche, F., 2, 4–5, 9, 18, 23, 24, 25, 44, 65, 78, 79, 80, 110, 120, 126–27, 145, 151, 163, 164
Nygren, A., 138

Ortega, J., 10, 12, 13, 27, 38, 39, 48, 52, 61, 90, 101, 141, 142, 144, 163

Otto, R., 17–18, 20

Paine, T., 8
Pascal, B., 139
Paul of Tarsus, 5, 30, 85, 139, 151
Peirce, C. S., 7, 27, 104, 106
Plotinus, 67
Poe, E. A., 18, 111

Rousseau, J.-J., 5, 131
Royce, J., 7, 28, 105, 140, 150

Santayana, G., 7, 10, 12, 15, 19, 24, 25, 31, 38, 54, 64, 66, 89, 105, 119, 161, 162, 163
Sartre, J.-P., 11, 38, 63, 65, 129, 136, 141, 163
Schiller, F., 126
Socrates, 112
Stekel, W., 163
Stirner, M., 163
Suzuki, D., 118
Swenson, D., 29

Unamuno, M., 22, 30, 36, 60, 124, 143, 152, 159, 162

Vasconcelos, J., 10, 40, 162
Vaz Ferreira, C., 143

Wagner, R., 108
Weber, M., 5
Whitehead, A., 10, 16, 17, 28, 31, 39, 68, 93, 129, 162

Subject Index

Alteración, 38–39, 48, 61
Art, 71, 88–91, 134–35, 154–55
Artistry, 88, 92, 93–94, 95, 97,
    114–15, 119–20
Availability, 153–57

Bhagavad-Gita, 19–20, 24, 40,
    41, 72, 92, 94
Body, 30, 62

Cathexis, 61–65, 71–72
Civilization, 8, 91–94, 99–100,
    133
Communion, 35–36, 132, 144–
    45, 156
Comprehensiveness, 14, 111
Contemplation, 58
Critical vitalism, 163–64

Desire, 62–63
Dream analysis, 60, 69, 70–73
Driving, 98–99, 120

Ensimismamiento, 39–40, 48, 112
Evaluation, 15–16, 55
Evil, 1–3, 74–75, 84; Augustin-
    ian, 3, 74; Manichaean, 2–3, 74
Expression, 56–57, 59
Externalization, 6, 164

Fear, 62–63, 66, 79–80
Feeling, 55
Fine art, 89–90, 107–10
Free association, 67–69, 78
Freedom, 11–13, 131, 143–44,
    153, 160
Free service, 138, 142
Fundamental arts, 95–99, 105
Futurity, 34–35

Hasidism, 32, 122–24, 126
Hatred, 2, 29, 37, 65–67, 74, 84,
    147–48, 158
Higher acceptance, 53–85

Identification, 58–61, 63, 71–72, 73

Inner check, 3, 83–84

Inward tolerance, 2–3, 80, 82–83

Leadership, 102–3

Leaping-ahead, 159

Leaping-in, 157–59

Life, 12, 27, 42; sense of, 17–18

Love, 93, 95, 129–60; sexual, 130–31

Loyalty, 150–53

Momentary experience, 31–35, 43

Mood, 23, 55–56

Over-ego, 51–54, 56, 61, 72, 74–75, 78, 81, 83–84, 90, 111–12

Pastness, 34

Personal existence, 26–31, 42–43, 50

Philosophy, 9–16, 23, 99, 110–14, 129–30, 162

Platonism, 23–24

Politics, 99–103

Presence, 31–33

Psychoanalysis, 61, 64, 68, 73–74, 77–78

Psychology, 9, 20–22, 42–43

Radical separation, 28–29, 129–30, 131–32, 139

Realism, 12–13

Reflection, 57

Reflective arts, 103–4

Reflexivity, 15–16, 112–13

Science, 104–6, 107

Self, 47–50, 139–40

Self-control, 53, 65, 81–85, 87–88, 95, 127–28

Sitting, 81, 88, 118–20

Song, 110–11

Substantive ego, 21, 32, 51–54, 56, 61, 71, 77, 78, 81, 83–84, 90, 118

Sufism, 32

Taoism, 120

Technology, 104–6

Trust, 147–50

Virtue, 4–6, 43–45, 87, 95, 114

Vivacious despair, 25

Zen, 32, 103, 116–24, 138